FEELING GOOD, FEELING BAD

Feeling Good, Feeling Bad

Dr. Diane Mandt Langberg

Servant Publications
Ann Arbor, Michigan

Scripture quotations taken from the New American
Standard Bible, © 1960, 1962, 1963, 1968, 1971, 1973, 1975,
1977 by The Lockman Foundation. Used by permission.

Published by Servant Publications
P.O. Box 8617
Ann Arbor, Michigan 48107

Cover design by Gerald Gawronski
ISBN 0-89283-713-6

91 92 93 94 95 10 9 8 7 6 5 4 3 2 1

Printed in the United States of America

Library of Congress Cataloging-in-Publication Data

Langberg, Diane Mandt.
   Feeling good, feeling bad / Diane Mandt Langberg.
      p. cm.
  ISBN 0-89283-713-6
  1. Women—Religious life. 2. Emotions—Religious aspects—
Christianity. 3. Women—Psychology. I. Title.
  BV4527.L28 1991
  248.8'43—dc20   91-4235

*Dedicated
to my parents,
whose love and courage
in the face of great hardship
has continually pointed me
to the ever-faithful One.*

Contents

Introduction

A GREAT DEAL OF CONFUSION and controversy exists regarding women today. A myriad of questions and conflicting answers increase the struggles and pressures many of us face. To write a book that so broadly addresses a multitude of issues has made me feel both overwhelmed and presumptuous; overwhelmed, because to cover any one topic thoroughly in a single chapter is impossible; presumptuous, because each woman's struggle is unique and the thought of ministering to her on paper and at a distance, is staggering.

Through many years as a counselor, I have, however, seen that much can be learned from considering a slice of a problem. Although each chapter deals with but one aspect of a particular problem, if you study it carefully you will grow both in your understanding of your own difficulties, as well as those of others. Volumes have been written about every area discussed here. Each subject has been narrowed by treating it as though I were responding to the struggles of a particular woman. Thus each topic is handled from a limited perspective.

The book—a manual, really—is not necessarily meant to be read all at once. Each chapter can be read as the need arises to find guidelines or perhaps just to stimulate thought as you consider a problem in your own life or in that of a loved one's or friend's. Oftentimes it may be beneficial to read two or three, as each covers a different but related problem (e.g., chapters 16, 17, and 37).

Much of what I have written has come out of the struggles of real women. *Many* have come to my office over the past twenty years of my practice with stories of pain and struggle. It has been a privilege to listen and walk alongside each of them. Often I have been their student. I have learned from their hurts and doubts, their fears and questions, as well as from their joys and hard-won growth. My hope is that this book will bring you treasures gleaned from these many lives.

As Christian women we are engaged in various battles that we fight in different arenas. For some the battlefield is our physical body; for others, it is the mind or emotions, and for many, it is relationships. And still others have difficulty with all four areas. Life in a fallen world means that each of us must struggle. God has, in Christ, equipped us for our battles, even as our bodies remain imperfect. This usually means that the struggles are not resolved instantaneously, but step by painful step—as we learn about our God, ourselves, and others.

God has called us to be strong and courageous, so that even in the midst of the battles he might be glorified. If the reading of these chapters encourages and challenges you on your particular battlefront, or helps you as you encourage another, then I will have accomplished my goal.

This book has truly been a community effort. I am, first of all, grateful to those women who have had the courage to come to my office and struggle with themselves and their lives in the presence of another. I treasure them beyond words. (It is important to note that the examples that I have used are not "lifted" from my practice, but, rather, are composite pictures used to illustrate a point.)

The book would not even exist had not the idea been born in the mind of my editor, Beth Feia, whose creativity and support I value greatly. She has been a pleasure to work with.

My family has endured with good humor and wonderful grace. My husband, Ron, picked up far more than his usual share of the load so I could keep my "dates" with the computer. My sons, Joshua and Daniel, have weathered schedule upsets, extra office time and store-bought cookies with good cheer. My mother-in-law, Vivian Langberg, who thought she had retired, spent hours editing chapters I could no longer think about clearly.

Isabelle Henard, with the sweetness of spirit that endears her to me, reworked the chapters and "made" the computer print them out properly. And so many other friends—where would I be without them? They offered time and ideas, encouragement and listening ears. How each enriches my life!

Please use this book merely as a jumping off point—not for complete solutions. It is my prayer that it will encourage you during dark times. Periods of struggle with ourselves and others are often puzzling and frustrating, "But we have this treasure in earthen vessels, that the surpassing greatness of the power may be of God and not from ourselves" (2 Corinthians 4:7).

Part One

A Woman
and Her Body

ONE

Do I Have PMS?

S UE HAS EXPERIENCED bloating, breast tenderness, cravings for sweets, and irritability prior to menstruation since she was an adolescent. Lately, these symptoms have worsened and Sue's husband has begun to react with frustration to his wife's "moody spells." Though Sue recognizes the toll that this has been taking on her marriage, she has not been able to contain her irritability.

Mary periodically feels depressed. Although she has never charted her moods, she suspects they are linked with her menstrual cycle, since she begins to feel better as soon as it is over.

Kim often suffers from cramping and headaches prior to menstruation. She feels overwhelmed, and says that these symptoms "just get to her" in a way other discomfort does not.

Many women have difficulties with depression and eating patterns prior to their periods, and would like information to determine whether their problem is caused by premenstrual syndrome (PMS). PMS is not easy to discuss with others, nor is it something women like to admit to. But having some information can help them evaluate the validity of their symptoms, and perhaps help deal with them in a better, less conflicted way.

PMS has sparked many years of debate among health professionals. Is PMS real, or does it exist only in a woman's mind? Is the cause truly physical, or simply an emotional response to hormonal change? There does seem to be consensus that PMS exists, but definitions vary. There is, however, general agreement about two aspects of PMS; the typical symptoms, and their timing in relation to the menstrual cycle.

PMS is characterized by its cyclical nature and accompanying symptoms, beginning usually one to ten days before menstruation and continuing until after the onset of menses. For some, however, symptoms can begin just after ovulation and continue until the end of the menstrual period. All patterns are followed by a symptom-free, intermediate phase lasting from a week to three weeks. This is clearly a different pattern from dysmenorrhea which *accompanies* the menstrual period, rather than preceding it.

PMS is thought to affect more than 70 percent of all women at some time during their childbearing years, but is most common during the twenties and thirties. Most who experience PMS have mild to moderate symptoms, with only a small percentage having severe symptoms.

The symptoms are usually grouped into three clusters: pain, edema, and psychological. The pain cluster usually consists of abdominal cramps, headaches, backaches, and muscle spasms, while the edema cluster includes breast tenderness, weight gain, swelling of extremities, bloating, abdominal heaviness, and pelvic pressure. The psychological manifestations include tension, irritability, depression, anxiety, and mood swings.

Since the timing and cyclical nature of symptoms are the central characteristics of PMS, it is useful to keep a careful daily diary of symptoms if you think you are experiencing this syndrome. It should be kept at least through one complete menstrual cycle, and preferably through three. Memory can be faulty, and recollections can be colored by the assumption that symptoms are related to your cycle when, in fact, they may be occurring sporadically throughout the month.

It is certainly true that some women use the symptoms, real or imagined, that accompany their menstrual cycles to avoid the stress of daily life for a few days. And it is true that being on the receiving end of these complaints is unpleasant. However, given the complicated nature of PMS, and all that is involved in its diagnosis, it is presumptuous to pass judgment on others as to whether or not their complaints are justified. Only the woman knows how severe her symptoms are and whether or not they are real. Often women who have milder symptoms are the harshest critics, because they believe that they "know" what the other woman is talking about, when in fact the difference in experience may be tremendous. Even in the case of someone who is using supposed symptoms as an excuse for withdrawing from life, the appropriate response is still empathy and compassion. Anyone who fears life and withdraws from its struggles needs our encouragement and support, not our judgment. Certainly this applies especially to those women whose symptoms are severe and sometimes life-controlling.

To determine whether you have this syndrome, you should first visit your gynecologist to discuss PMS more thoroughly and get specific instructions on how to keep a chart of your symptoms. It is the only way to get an accurate diagnosis. Second, follow your doctor's treatment plan to see if that alleviates any of your symptoms. Your doctor may recommend a carefully monitored diet to make it easier to cope with stress. Often the diet is less than ideal during many women's cycles, as they tend to crave sweets and eat accordingly. It is also helpful to cut down on sodium to reduce water retention, and on sugar and caffeine to alleviate tension and irritability. Another important tool is exercise, which can alleviate symptoms such as depression, tension, anxiety, fatigue, and irritability. Finally, some physicians recommend vitamin B6 supplements. Although many women report relief when taking them, they should be used with caution because B6 in high doses has been reported to be toxic. By using these methods to alleviate physical distress, and by gaining a thorough understanding of your symptoms and how they relate to your cycle, you will be able to anticipate bad days and plan around them.

A note of caution about two destructive attitudes in regard to yourself and to others. The first is that it is important not to be defensive about your premenstrual experiences. The judgmental responses of others—physicians, family members, friends—can make you defensive—as if they think you have made it all up, that your opinions are not valid when you are premenstrual, or that you have some silly female flaw they must tolerate until you "get over it." Do not allow such reactions to keep you from finding a doctor with whom you are comfortable, who will help you chart your symptoms, and who—if the diagnosis is PMS—will respond in a way that does not attack your self-esteem or credibility.

At the same time it is important not to respond in derogatory ways to women who share these struggles. While we do not want to encourage complaining and whining in others, we do not want to attack their self-esteem or credibility either. We are never equipped to judge the internal physical, emotional, or spiritual experiences of another with complete accuracy.

Another destructive and extreme attitude to guard against is, of course, using PMS as an excuse to avoid life. I am always struck by the harmony in Jesus' response to us in difficulty. He never fails to sympathize with our weaknesses; he remembers that we are but dust. However, he also calls upon us, and enables us, to face life with courage even in the midst of pain. We need to strive for that same harmony in our attitudes toward both others and ourselves.

TWO

How Will Pregnancy Affect Me?

I F THERE IS ONE ROLE UNIQUE TO A WOMAN, it is that of becoming a mother. The church, society, and women themselves have seen childbearing as the culminating event in a woman's life. Whether or not this is so, it clearly leads to tremendous expectations about pregnancy, delivery, and raising a child. Very little, if any, systematic research has been carried out concerning women's motivations for becoming pregnant, which is surprising if you think about it.

Ideally, a woman wants a child because she loves her husband, wants to create a new life with him, likes children, enjoys nurturing them, and sees motherhood as an important role in life. God himself has called upon her to be fruitful and multiply!

Couples have a wide variety of unexpressed, and perhaps unconscious, reasons for having children. Kay and Harry, for example, have been married for several years. Although things seem fine in the relationship, Kay is aware that Harry has been spending more time away from home. She thinks that having a child might draw him back. She also hopes that the responsibilities of fatherhood will cause Harry to be more attentive to their marriage.

Then there's Mary and Lonnie. Shortly after their honeymoon ended, they began to quarrel with increasing frequency. Recently each has had doubts about having chosen to marry the other. Each is secretly fearful the marriage won't last. But maybe if they had a child? Perhaps a baby would cement their relationship.

The reasons women themselves want to become pregnant are myriad. Many crave the love and dependency of another human being. Others feel that having a child is the ultimate of creative acts—that it will not only raise their own self-esteem, but their status in the eyes of others. Sometimes, as has already been said, a woman may feel that a child will strengthen the tenuous bond between herself and her husband. Perhaps the most widespread notion is that a child can provide a new beginning; a perfect person into whom can be poured all her hopes and expectations—particularly those she hasn't fulfilled in her own life. And finally, there is the belief that having children, creating a family, is the natural thing to do.

As you may see, some of these motives do not provide the best beginning for the child. They also put great strain on the marriage. If you are ambivalent, why don't you and your husband try to sort through, as honestly as you can, why you want to have a child at this time? Buttress your conversations with much prayer together. Ask God to show you your hearts. Ask for his wisdom as to when to start your family. God's word tells us that the days ordained for your child are already written in his book! How wonderful that you can trust him to guide you!

This perspective can guide not only your decision about becoming pregnant, but your attitude toward your pregnancy and the rearing of your child as well. Life changes usually bring ambivalence, but ambivalence is not wrong of itself. Ambivalence can be overcome through prayer and a search for God's wisdom. There is much we as parents cannot control, and God alone can see the future. Thus, reliance on the wisdom of God is essential. Raising a human being created in the image of God is both a serious and joyful responsibility.

Each woman's pregnancy is different, even as it is the same. What will this experience do to you physically? Have you been an active person, involved in a career? Do you have concerns about the physical and emotional changes that pregnancy will bring? A thorough understanding of the trimesters and the development of your baby can be gleaned from many excellent books available in almost any bookstore. As you anticipate these changes and learn the reasons for them, both you *and* your husband will become excited and awed that you are bringing a new being into the world together.

Coping with change, even good change, causes stress. Your body may be experiencing things you have never felt before such as: nausea, changes in appetite, fatigue, and a decrease or increase in sex drive. Depending on how your body reacts, your lifestyle may have to be altered somewhat. And if pregnancy does not alter your lifestyle, having a child certainly will. Your emotions may range from calm to agitation.

If you are used to perceiving yourself as self-sufficient, you may be surprised to find yourself needing help during pregnancy, childbirth, and the early post-partum weeks. You may feel some anxiety as you become more dependent on your husband. Your ability to trust him is an important factor in your sense of security, because you will need his support, both emotionally and physically, in ways that have not been necessary before.

Though your husband's body will not be undergoing the changes that yours will, he will be dealing with changes of his own. You may not only be acting differently, your appearance will definitely be different. He may feel hurt as your pregnancy draws to a close and your focus shifts more to the baby, and away from him. This is also true in the early postpartum weeks. If you experience a decrease in sex drive, his feelings of hurt and rejection may be even greater. Therefore, it is crucial that both you and your husband be aware that he too will be coping with change. Sensitivity to his needs, and mutual consideration for the needs of each other are so important during this time. The toll new parenthood takes on your marriage will be determined in large measure by your responsiveness to each other. Though these changes can cause a rift in your marriage, they can also become a means of drawing together, of enhancing your relationship in a deep way. It is a memorable time, and one that can bring you both great joy.

There is no reason that a pregnant woman cannot be fit. The better you care for yourself, the healthier your baby and most probably, the easier your labor and delivery will be. Just do not get the mistaken notion that fit means thin! On the other hand, pregnancy is no excuse to eat everything in sight. A well-balanced diet, combined with consistent and appropriate exercise, is crucial to a healthy pregnancy.

You and your husband can use every step toward parenthood to draw closer to God and to each other. Both relationships must be strong if you are to nurture each other and the child you will bring into the world. Do not expect it to be easy. Do not expect it to be without pain. But do anticipate it with great joy.

THREE

I Love My Baby—So Why Am I Depressed?

M OTHERHOOD OFTEN comes as quite a shock.
Through our experiences in school, relationships, and careers we come to view ourselves in particular ways. As children living in a world of adults, we learn to evaluate ourselves based on adult feedback. In school, we discover we are competent when we get good grades. In relationships, we realize we are successful when people show they like us. In our careers, our efforts bring promotions and praise. All of these feedbacks work together not only to give us a sense of who we are, but also to help us value ourselves. Rightly or wrongly, our self-worth is often determined by the input of others.

One of the great shocks of motherhood is that suddenly no one is on hand to offer input—unless you count the crying in the middle of the night and endless dirty diapers!

Recently Jane told me of her disappointment in herself at not experiencing the joy she anticipated with the birth of her first child, but of actually feeling depressed. Having been a successful professional for ten years, and having planned and eagerly awaited the birth of her baby, she now felt, four months later, constantly exhausted and uninterested in sex. She was not eating well, and, perhaps worst of all, felt guilty for being so unhappy at what should have been a thrilling time.

Unreasonable as these feelings may seem, they are not unusual. Perhaps you have had a similar experience. You have just spent nine months being pregnant. Your body has undergone extreme changes. Your hormones have flip-flopped. You probably didn't sleep well the last two months of your pregnancy. In all likelihood, you carried on in your job until near delivery. Then, tired and bulky, your body exerted a tremendous effort, and, possibly with intense pain, your baby was born. Your hormones changed again, and you were sent home, exhausted and sore, with a totally dependent infant, who now is waking often throughout the night and seems to eat constantly. Your body is attempting to recuperate, with little rest, as you care for a helpless, sometimes unpredictable baby, who totally controls your schedule.

Your life has been changing both inside and outside. You have left a full-time job. You have been used to a fast-paced day with constant interactions with colleagues, in work which required you to be alert and articulate, and kept you in constant contact with other alert and articulate adults. You may have been required to read and research, to be involved in debate, to analyze data, with your verbal skills held at a premium. Your days followed a relatively predictable and controllable schedule, with room for personal desires and space. But now, your days are completely controlled by another human being whom you cannot ignore. In the work world you were goal-oriented and were given tangible rewards for a job well done. Now your tasks are repetitive, done for an infant you think is incapable of showing any appreciation for your undivided attention.

The contrast between the two scenarios is clear, but the purpose in contrasting them is not to say that being at home with an infant is full of negatives, or that the career world is full of positives. This is certainly not the case. The point is that the life you were used to is abruptly gone. In its place is an entirely new one. Former ways of coping, of taking care of yourself, no longer apply. You have been thrust into a different set of circumstances, and, while the old coping mechanisms do not work, new ones have not yet been developed.

Let's look at some of the more difficult aspects of your life today, and then at some ideas for handling them.

Monotony is a common frustration for new mothers, as well as for mothers of small children. Children need routines because they give them a sense of security. Your days consist of responding to your baby's need for the routines of sleeping, waking, feeding, diapering, and nurturing. After attending to round one of those needs, round two promptly begins. Every job, of course, has boring routines, but most provide more stimulation than a new mother receives alone with her child at home. Your child will bring more variety into your life as he gets older and can do more. In the meantime, however, you will have to insure that you have activities—both with your child and apart from him or her—that you find stimulating. When women do not do this, they often become depressed and lethargic. Not only are they bored, they become boring!

A sense of isolation is another difficulty for mothers of young children. Depending on your neighborhood, this happens to a greater or lesser degree. Your friends and colleagues through work are no longer part of your daily circle. Seek out new friends whose lives are more similar to yours to keep loneliness from overwhelming you. Do not stay home alone with your child, day after day. An infant is made to be carried, so carry him—to involve yourself with other young mothers at your church, or in your neighborhood. Ask your husband to assist you, so you can have friends in your home that you both enjoy. Keep it simple and end it early! Don't assume you can entertain in the same way, or keep the same hours as you did before.

Last, but certainly not least, a major complaint of young mothers is fatigue. Irregular hours, little sleep, and the many changes mentioned earlier may result in overwhelming tiredness. I have heard many young mothers say they can hardly imagine *not* being tired. They are often annoyed with themselves, remembering the time when they juggled a full-time career, a home, a marriage, and daily exercise without exhaustion. "What's wrong with me? I barely have the energy to take care of one infant!" However, the responsibility for that little one requires a very different kind of activity that is also constant, not familiar, and complicated by the fact that their bodies are still recuperating.

Not eating properly, a common practice at this demanding time, can also greatly increase your fatigue. A healthy diet and regular exercise can help combat depression. It is hard to imagine managing either when you are feeling depressed, so start gradually. Eat small amounts more frequently. Ask your husband to watch the baby while you take a short walk every day.

Fatigue, too, can reduce your sex drive, as can nursing your baby. Although not all lactating women are affected this way, many are. While nursing, you tend not to lubricate as well, too, and that can be a discouragement. In this area, as in all the others, the more support and encouragement you get from your husband, the better.

Try not to waste your time feeling guilty about this period of personal growth. Remember that you are going through a tremendous transition and time is needed for you to get your bearings. Talk at length with your husband about your feelings and needs. Ask him to help you. Sharing your thoughts and affection with each other can be a great support.

If after trying these suggestions you find no relief from depression, seek counseling to better understand yourself and this season of your life. God has indeed blessed you, but that lovely gift from him requires big changes on your part. Even good change is often hard. In time you will develop ways of handling your new-found difficulties, which in turn will enable you to thoroughly enjoy your new-found blessings!

FOUR

Am I Wrong to Feel So Sad about My Miscarriage?

MISCARRIAGE IS MUCH MORE COMMON than most people realize. Studies have shown that 15 to 20 percent of known pregnancies end in spontaneous abortion. It is also a much more emotionally devastating experience than has previously been acknowledged. The silence that surrounds the experience, coupled with many misunderstandings, can result in deep grief, profound guilt, and a fear of subsequent pregnancies. Even though both husband and wife may experience depression, often it is the woman who suffers inordinately. Friends tell her that the loss was probably caused by some defect in the fetus, and that she should be grateful that the pregnancy ended this way. Their inability to share her grief increases her sense of isolation.

Let's consider some facts about miscarriage before we look at the emotional experience the couple is undergoing. Not only do up to 20 percent of pregnancies end in miscarriage, but the risk increases with the advancing age of a woman. With more and more women waiting until later in life to start a family, miscarriages have become more common. Although in over 50 percent of the cases, the fetus is anatomically or genetically abnormal, the accompanying

17

guilt is often rooted in many of the myths that surround miscarriage. "If I hadn't moved the furniture, or played tennis, or made love with my husband, this never would have happened." On the contrary, minor trauma and normal physical exertion seldom interrupt a normal, healthy pregnancy. Because couples do not receive this reassurance, they may experience unnecessary fear and guilt. Obviously, they need to consult with a gynecologist to obtain a diagnosis of the actual cause.

If you have experienced a miscarriage, perhaps knowing these things may allay your irrational feelings of guilt, but it clearly will not eliminate the emotional pain. Both you and your husband would be wise to have an open and thorough discussion with your physician to understand what has happened, so that your sadness is not complicated by a misunderstanding of the physical facts. Beyond that, recognize your experience as a genuine and justifiable grief reaction. Any loss in life is a kind of death, and death is painful and difficult to face. It is made more difficult when that death is not acknowledged by those around us. In struggling with your feelings about the miscarriage, you may also be struggling with the lack of support from your friends. What could you and your husband do to ease this very real pain?

First, realize that both of you are facing a death. Whenever we face a death, we deal with reactions such as denial, anger, and sorrow in the process of becoming reconciled to our loss. These are feelings both you and your husband may experience, whether or not others give them any credibility. Find a friend, pastor, or counselor who can help you. Hospitals often have groups for those who have had a miscarriage which are led by women who have undergone the same experience. Your hospital or doctor can put you in touch with such groups. You will find it helpful to have your feelings and fears validated by others, rather than denied or made light of. To deny your feelings is to bury them deeply, rather than to allow them to heal.

In my years of counseling, women in their fifties and six-
ties have come to me because of the great sadness they still
bear over a miscarried child. That grief was never discussed
or resolved, and has therefore turned into bitterness and
depression as the years have gone by. For this reason, resolution of your grief soon after your miscarriage is of great
importance. When you consider another pregnancy, you do
not want the joy of expecting a new baby to be overridden
by fear and guilt that you have not resolved. Grieving over
the miscarriage will also assure that the next child will not be
regarded as a replacement for the lost one, even unconsciously. That certainly would be a terrible burden to put on
your new baby.

Frequently the husband is not considered a primary
player in a miscarriage. Often his feelings are ignored, perhaps because a man is less likely to allow himself to feel and
express sadness. Granted, his body has not undergone
changes, nor has he experienced the physical loss his wife
has. However, his loss is just as real. He, too, participated in
creating the child. He, too, looked forward to a new baby
and has had those expectations crushed. If your husband is
able to acknowledge his depression, you will be able to
resolve your grief as a couple. Too often the wife considers
herself as the only one facing loss, and the husband is left
out. The grieving needs to be done together. A wife's loss
may be different from the husband's, but both are real.

While acknowledging your husband's loss, you should
realize that his experience is different from yours. Because
personalities differ, the way each of you grieves is not likely
to be the same. One of you may need to talk about the experience over and over again to get a handle on it, while the
other one may need to talk a little, but then will require time
alone to sort things out. The difference in grieving styles can
cause a rift between even the most devoted couple. The quiet
one may see the other as persisting in stirring up painful
memories, while the more verbal one mistakes silence for

rejection and an unwillingness to face sadness. In reality, each is simply handling grief in the way that is most healing for his or her personality. Your ability to respond to each other may be limited since each is struggling with his or her own pain. You would probably be more available to each other in a different situation, when only one of you was facing a problem. You also need to share with someone besides your spouse—a friend, a pastor, or perhaps even better, a couple in your church who has dealt with the same problem. If not one of these, then a few sessions with a counselor would be of benefit.

Remember that your loss is real, your pain is real. Neither is imagined. Give yourselves time for the work of grieving to be complete before you attempt another pregnancy. This may take a full year. The miscarriage is not your fault, nor is it a punishment from God. Carry with you the words of the psalmist; "Just as a father has compassion on his children, so the Lord has compassion on those who fear Him. For He Himself knows our frame; He is mindful that we are but dust" (Psalm 103:13-14). As God is compassionate and patient with you, be compassionate and patient with yourself, confident that healing will come to both you and your husband.

FIVE

I'm Afraid I Can't Have Children!

A BOUT FIFTEEN PERCENT OF MARRIED COUPLES in the United States have problems with infertility. Although this is usually seen as a "female" problem, 40 percent of the time, the problem is with the husband. In any case, it is important to remember that two persons share the difficulty. Conception depends on the fertility of each, and help is needed by both when infertility is a problem for either. Attempting to deal with infertility without medical help is not wise, particularly after one year of attempting to conceive without success. Let's look at some examples.

After three years of marriage Nancy and Mark were ready to begin a family. Nancy looked forward to motherhood and had watched many of her friends happily enter this new role. Some had begun to make comments like, "Not pregnant yet, Nancy? You don't know what you're missing!" She and Mark had stopped using birth control almost a year ago. Was something wrong? What if she couldn't get pregnant? How could she face such a sorrow? How would she feel around her friends? She wouldn't fit in! Pregnancy consumed her thoughts. She became fearful about her future, if there were no children in it.

It is natural, after a certain point in marriage, to want to have children. To reach the stage where you are surrounded by others who are beginning their families, and to find yourself unable to conceive, is painful indeed. It is also frightening to think that something might be wrong with you. Often women feel guilty, and dredge up things in their past—illicit sex in previous relationships, premarital sex with their husband, an abortion—as possible causes of infertility. They may conclude that God must be punishing them for some real or imagined sin by depriving them of this kind of fulfillment. When these emotions are coupled with the felt criticism of others, the pain and accompanying loneliness can be unbearable.

Acquaintances may believe, as many women themselves do, that God's ultimate purpose for them is to have babies. Is God's ideal woman a mother? The belief that women were put on earth to have children has always been strong in Christian society and seems now to have come into vogue again as an over-reaction to the feminist movement and the deterioration of the American family. Many current books suggest a reasoning that goes something like this: "God says be fruitful and multiply and any woman who is not doing this with abandon is either disobedient to God's command, or at the very least is sadly missing out on God's best for her life."

That puts all unmarried women in a crippling position, and also condemns single and infertile women to a half-fulfilled life, no matter what else they do. Furthermore, it leaves no room for God to call some couples, either by choice or design, to remain childless. I personally see no evidence in Scripture that God has called *all* women, for *all* time, to exactly the same role or mission. I do not see anywhere in Scripture a blueprint for The Ideal Woman. Paul himself suggests that the unmarried state is best. It is also clear from Jesus' interactions with women that he did not view them as walking wombs and breasts. Beyond being courteous to them, he revealed spiritual truths to them, and gave them important responsibilities. When we suggest that God's best is not available for celibate or childless women, we are adding to Scripture and also to the burden that these women may already carry.

If you are unable to have children, do not allow the judgments and faulty opinions of others to diminish your relationship with God. Jesus encouraged Mary, against the tradition of his day—which allowed no place for women at the feet of a teacher—to "choose that good part." There is a higher calling than tradition and that is to sit at his feet and hear from him regarding each situation in life as it occurs. If you are anxious about infertility, Jesus would have you sit at *his* feet, not the feet of popular opinion. God's ideal woman is not a mother, but a person who has the courage to follow him, and strive to be like him regardless of circumstances.

As you remain open to God, there are some positive steps you can take. First, as you work through your own sadness and fears, and pursue testing and medical help, try to avoid making fertility and pregnancy the central focus of your lives or of conversations with friends. You will continually be waiting for test results and wondering. You will count days each month and wait for your cycle to begin, hoping against hope that it will not. While this may be unavoidable, it is crucial even as it is difficult, to have time both with your husband and others that offsets your anxiety.

Develop friendships with couples who have no children. Pursue a common interest together, so that there may be a different foundation for your friendship. Find a happy place to relax and have fun, where other things can occupy your mind and your conversation. And, when you feel comfortable saying it, let your friends know what you are going through, and of your need for your times together not to focus around that struggle.

In your lovemaking, determine with your husband that it will not always be centered on getting pregnant. For many couples, lovemaking is reduced to a means to an end, and the strain on the relationship is great. It is all too easy for each to feel used by the other. The oasis that sex is meant to be is then gone at a time when you need it most. Perhaps you can create a respite by taking a month off now and then from temperature taking and other preventative measures just to enjoy each other again. Or, make sure a week or more every month is spent without your preoccupation of doing all these things. As much as your budget will allow, go off somewhere quiet and relaxing together for fun. Obviously, this will have to take into account what your doctor has recommended, but in your earnestness, do not forget to play together.

What I am about to say may seem to contradict the above; you both need to find place and time where you *can* discuss your feelings and fears. It is vital, especially during times of stress, to keep your communication with each other open, understanding, and supportive. On the other hand, you cannot be the only outlet for each other, because this would put too great a strain on your relationship. Each of you needs other outlets as well. One possibility is for each of you to keep a journal to chronicle your thoughts, your reactions, your questions, and uncertainties. A personal journal is helpful to get a healthy perspective, because it permits utter freedom of expression, with no fear of judgment or criticism. As the journal unfolds, you will see how you have grown, how your thinking has changed. Your journal can become the record of a journey that you will treasure in the future.

Another possible outlet is for each of you to have a close friend who will commit himself or herself to be there as listener, supporter, shoulder, even mirror. Such a friend can be there in ways that you and your husband cannot be for each other, because he or she is not an actual participant. You do not need someone who will tell you what to do, or criticize what you are already doing, but rather someone who will be a strong ally. If you cannot find such a person (and they are rare indeed!), seek out a professional counselor.

Maintaining a healthy perspective on the problem, on your marriage, and on yourself will be difficult in the midst of all you are handling, and most people need help.

In conclusion, to repeat; keep in mind that the focus of your life is not whether you have a baby. Nor is it whether you measure up to the opinions others have of God's ideal woman. The most important thing is that you continue, day after day, to "choose that good part," and that, in spite of your fears and questions, you glorify God, because you are a woman who is determined to be like Jesus.

SIX

Menopause Has Come: What's Happening to Me?

THE STEREOTYPE OF THE MENOPAUSAL WOMAN certainly inspires justified trepidation for anyone approaching it. She is told to expect not only to beware of hot flashes, but of being tired, grumpy, depressed, hard to live with, over-weight—*and* sexually unattractive! Unfortunately, this negative image of what should and can be a normal time can turn into a self-fulfilling prophecy. If a woman expects menopause to mean loss of interest in sex, it probably will. If she anticipates physical deterioration, she will be less likely to take good care of herself. "Why fight it?" And expecting to be tired and lacking in creativity, she may begin to stagnate. But is this really inevitable?

The answer requires some understanding of menopause itself. Simply put, menopause is the end of menstruation. The ovaries, which produce estrogen and release eggs for possible fertilization, gradually slow down their production of hormones after the age of twenty-five. The diminution is very gradual until around the ages of forty-five to fifty-two, when noticeable changes begin to occur. A woman may find her periods to be irregular, not only in timing but in amount of flow. In time, usually several years, her periods will completely stop. Sometimes they will cease abruptly. Menopause is said to be over after a full year with no periods. This can happen as early as age forty-five, or as late as sixty.

Two main symptoms are linked to the hormonal changes of menopause. The degree of their severity is not predictable, though about seventy-five percent of women say they have experienced them in some measure. The first is hot flashes, which are feelings of extreme heat in the upper part of the body, sometimes accompanied by drenching sweats, the result of instability in the blood vessels. Although hot flashes can be very uncomfortable, sometimes embarrassing, and often interrupting one's sleep, they are not usually disruptive of normal activities or of a feeling of well-being. If you should find them intolerable your gynecologist may recommend supplemental hormones. Current research is showing that there may be many benefits to women who take hormones during menopause, but it is a decision to be made between a woman and her physician.

The second physical effect of menopause is thinning and drying of the vaginal wall, which can cause discomfort in intercourse and also be a factor in urinary tract infections. Painful intercourse can be alleviated by a water-soluble lubricant. Aside from this possible discomfort, which can be overcome, there is nothing about menopause that should reduce your enjoyment of sexual activity. Some debate exists over whether the body's reduced level of the hormone estrogen results in diminished interest in sex. The biggest predictor, however, is the sexual pattern a woman and her husband have had before menopause. If she enjoyed her sexual relationship before menopause, she will more than likely enjoy it after. For many women, the quality of their sex life improves when there is no longer fear of pregnancy or concern with contraception.

Studies have shown there is no higher percentage of hospitalization for depression during menopause than any other time in a woman's life, despite the supposed link. What has been shown is that those women who had low self-esteem and were dissatisfied before menopause were more likely to experience depression during and after menopause. So again, as with the sexual area, the greatest predictor seems to be your perspective before entering menopause. A woman who has been reasonably happy, both in and out of her marriage should continue to enjoy a full and satisfying life.

Perhaps more significant than physical changes is the emotional component of menopause, since it usually occurs during an important period of transition in the lives of most women. The physical considerations of menopause can be exacerbated by the reality that a woman's focus is shifting from home and children to a life of greater freedom. This can be a frightening or joyful prospect. For women who have never had children, acceptance that any chance is now over, can bring great sadness. The loss of fertility is difficult for most women, even those who don't want more children, because it seems to whisper, "You're getting old!" And it can be especially intense for single women who have longed for homes and motherhood. But for those women who have not defined themselves in any way other than wife and mother, menopause can also be very scary. They may feel a productive life means producing children, so the main purpose of their lives is over, which can result in severe depression.

Keep in mind that any change—even good change—can be difficult. If change involves departure from the only area in which you feel competent, of course it will be upsetting! Remember what has been said earlier in this book; God does not define a woman simply in terms of her ability to give birth and be a mother. Every woman is his daughter, created in his image, gifted by him for the good of his body. For many women, a large portion of their lives involves expressing that in the arena of the home. As any single woman can testify, there are many other places besides homes to do this. As home demands less of a woman, her response should *not* be, "My mission in life is over. I'm not of value anymore."

Rather, "I've worked hard to glorify God in one arena. Now I have the freedom to look for another."

For women who have not had children, their sense of loss may take more time to overcome. However, these women can remind themselves of the same thing; there are many ways to be fruitful, and having children is only one of them.

The ability to reproduce is a blessing, but it is only one of many God gives. The psalmist expresses it beautifully; "How blessed is the man who does not walk in the counsel of the wicked, nor stand in the path of sinners, nor sit in the seat of scoffers! But his delight is in the law of the Lord... he will be like a tree firmly planted by streams of water, which yields its fruit in its season, and its leaf does not wither; and in whatever he does, he prospers" (Psalm 1:1-3).

Whether or not you have enjoyed bearing the fruit of children before menopause, look forward now to yielding a different fruit in a different season.

SEVEN

What's Good about Celibacy?

S EX IS CERTAINLY GETTING A LOT OF ATTENTION lately, isn't it? I do wonder how people were ever able to sell anything, before the use of sex in marketing. It's bad enough we're bombarded with such advertising, but worse, it suggests that without sex we'll lead miserable, unfulfilled lives. That pushes us to pursue sexual expression without let up. And if we're not successful, we're not getting what we deserve; which pushes us harder.

The biblical view clearly is that single Christians should be celibate. But what exactly is celibacy? It is abstention from sexual activity *by choice*, a conscious and deliberate decision. This is a very important point. So often Christian singles view celibacy as something forced upon them, but true celibacy is not. Just as a married Christian chooses to obey God through fidelity, an unmarried Christian chooses to obey through celibacy. *Both* celibacy and fidelity are continual choices. To make a commitment to either we must choose to abandon the alternative. Furthermore, the choice should not be made out of necessity or under duress.

Celibacy is not a curse that God has placed on singles. All Christians are called to be disciples, but the paths we walk may be different. Some are called to be a disciple through celibacy, some through marriage, some through parenting. God's emphasis (unlike the world's) is not on sex itself, but on whether we are living in a way that brings honor to his name. Obviously, sexual expression can come and go in our lives, since a first call may be to celibacy, then shift to marriage. Or the reverse may be true, when the end of a marriage may abruptly call us to celibacy. The overriding directive in a Christian's life is not to have sexual fulfillment, or to be married, or even to have children. Nor is it to have a successful and fulfilling career. The central directive is that God should be glorified. Circumstances are secondary to our purpose, which is to glorify God. Basic to doing that, for a single person, is to choose celibacy.

Singles have handled this in a variety of ways. Some have asked God to remove their need or desire for sex. But God created men and women as sexual beings. Was God, who became the man Jesus, a sexual being? The author of Hebrews says, "Therefore, He had to be made like His brethren in all things, that He might become a merciful and faithful high priest in things pertaining to God, to make propitiation for the sins of the people. For since He Himself was tempted in that which He has suffered, He is able to come to the aid of those who are tempted" (Hebrews 2:17-18).

Jesus knows what it means to be a sexual being and yet be without sexual fulfillment, particularly since he too lived in a culture that disapproved of singleness. Did Jesus deny and repress his sexuality? Or did he have the courage to face his sexual drives and then to *choose* celibacy as a means of glorifying God?

We all face limitations; it is our nature to collide with and resent them. If I marry one man, I have, by virtue of my choice, excluded all others. If I choose one job, then I cannot perform another I might also want to do. If I order fish for dinner, then I am choosing not to have steak. Obviously some choices are more life-defining and permanent than others. But let us not fall for the popular expression: "If you feel like doing it, do it!" It is false that we do not have to operate within limits, that we have the right to have whatever we want, whenever we want it.

As a celibate, study and act upon your gifts and abilities to give purpose to your life. Obviously this is important for those who are married as well. Unfortunately, even churches have often communicated that living alone is living a half-life. However, the whole (and holy) life depends on living *out* what God has put *in*.

As a celibate, do not deny your sexuality. God has not given sexuality only to those who marry. It is a core part of any person's identity. To deny its existence will be to function as less than God has intended. It is expressed in your warmth toward others and your love toward others of both sexes. Sexuality is not just expressed in the sexual act itself. It touches all that you do because you were created to be a sexual being. Every aspect of your relationship is affected by it.

Recognize, too, that, though a sexual being, your physical urges do not have to control your life. All of who we are is to be submitted to God: our bodies, our hearts, our minds. Self-control is a gift from God and every aspect of our lives requires the exercising of that gift. Celibacy is but another way of exercising self-control through making the right choice.

To be celibate for the wrong reasons would be a position taken from weakness, not from the strength that God intends for us to have. Too many single people choose celibacy out of fear of the opposite sex or of intimacy, or even the fear of making a marriage commitment. Celibacy is a strength when it is chosen out of obedience to God, and a recognition that he has called you to it, at least for now. It becomes a strength when it glorifies God.

To develop good strong relationships with the opposite sex, try not to think of your relationships only in terms of whether they will lead to marriage. Too many men and women know little about how to relate as friends. They may know how to date, or how to behave in a hierarchical way, such as boss to secretary. Think about how you go about developing a good friendship with a person of your own sex. What do you look for? How do you build that relationship? Certainly in a male-female relationship sexuality will have to be dealt with, consciously or unconsciously. Sexuality denied tends to escalate, to the detriment of the friendship.

God's laws are not arbitrary, but purposeful. His limits are not punishments, but protection. We all must seek to understand the wisdom of his laws, of his limits, whether in regard to sexuality, or anything else. Choosing God's way is not a one-time thing, but a choice we must make over and over again. When you pursue his way, you will find yourself loving others and being loved.

EIGHT

Memories of Incest Haunt Me

TARA CAME TO ME IN HER MID-TWENTIES, suddenly flooded by memories she had totally forgotten—memories of things too horrible to accept at the time—memories of a sexual relationship with her father from the age of four until she was eighteen. Now that those scars have been reopened, she can hardly function. She awakens at night, trembling from nightmares, and even wishing for death to put an end to her agony.

Karen, on the other hand, has never forgotten her incestuous relationship with her grandfather. She's been depressed for years, has never been able to maintain long-term relationships with men, and has trouble making decisions.

Incest sounds shocking, almost melodramatic. Yet one in four women and one in six men are sexually abused before the age of eighteen. These statistics cut across educational, socio-economic, and religious lines. Because of the severe trauma that incest causes, it is not unusual that Tara experienced amnesia for so long, until her memories were triggered by some external event—perhaps a television program, a movie, or a conversation. The result was bound to be overwhelming pain, fear, anger, and depression. Recalling such memories, Tara and others like her suddenly feel their lives are out of control, that they can't function even routinely. However many, too, are like Karen. They have never forgotten, but they have never talked with anyone about it.

The first step an incest victim must take is to break the silence that has isolated her. Though always extremely difficult, it is a step toward healing and recovery. Most who have been abused as children have never told anyone, for good reason. Their attempts to report the abuse when they were younger elicited responses which imposed blame, or threats and name-calling, and were usually accompanied by absolute denial. Even trying to tell of it years later as adults, they may sense rejection in the horror others feel, and come away with feelings of shame. Families themselves may go to great trouble to protect the perpetrators among them, rather than liberate the victims, because they are loathe to admit such aberrant behavior exists among them. Though the trauma of incest is terrible, it is the repression of the trauma that causes even greater damage.

But, in spite of this, it is vital to tell someone about the situation, and it is equally vital to tell someone in a safe place. Verbalizing your experience is healing when the person who hears reacts with respect and caring. Usually this is a therapist with experience in counseling victims of incest.

The second thing that must be understood is that healing is really possible, even though it is long and hard. Christians are often naive about the effects of sin. They seem to think that if we acknowledge sin and believe God can heal it, we will soon be all right. This may be true about some experiences. But when a central figure in our lives whom we expected to be trustworthy has abused us during our formative years, the effects are bound to be of long duration. You as an incest victim have no reason to feel guilty, to deny the pain you feel, or to apologize for the time required for you to understand the hurt and be healed. The fact that it will take time is not a negative reflection on you.

When telling others your story, you will wrestle with depression, low self-esteem, and dissatisfaction with life in general and yourself in particular. You may feel anxious, helpless, and even paralyzed when trying to act. You will experience intense anger. This is positive anger, because it is warranted anger. God hates sin, and he too is angry about what happened to you. Sometimes a victim is so terrified of the anger felt toward the abuser that she becomes self-mutilating or self-destructive. Unresolved anger may also lead to addictions, or even to suicidal thoughts and attempts. All are rooted in anger which needs to be expressed.

We often feel uncomfortable venting intense anger, especially against someone we feel an obligation to love and respect. Rather than expressing it, we may handle it by turning it inward, especially if we already carry strong feelings of unworthiness. Persons who have been abused erroneously see themselves as deserving punishment and rejection.

A therapist—preferably a Christian one—can provide a safe haven for verbalizing your justified anger and freeing you from it. Christian or not, the counselor must be someone you can trust. Perhaps it was the most important man in your childhood who proved not to be trustworthy. He was not there for you in good ways; moreover, he abused you when you were too young and dependent to defend yourself. The counselor is a key to relearning how to trust. And, if the counselor is a Christian, you will be helped to place your ultimate trust in God.

Blame is a strong thread that will run through all your hard work. Abused children—no matter what the form of abuse—invariably take the blame upon themselves. This blame is frequently reinforced by messages given by the abusing adult. "You asked for it!" "If you weren't so naughty I wouldn't have to keep doing this." "I'm doing this for your own good!" If a child discovers a central figure in her life cannot be trusted, then that means her world is not a safe place. This results in a kind of paralysis, causing the child to withdraw. Persons are not safe, school is not safe, church is not safe. "The world may be safe for others, but there must be something wrong with me or this would not have happened."

Remember that incest is a criminal act by someone else, *not* you. You did not ask for it, you did not bring it on yourself. You must remember that even if you believe you participated, you consented only to gain and keep love. Little children cannot protect themselves, and they are deprived when their God-given families fail to protect them. Circumstances do *not* validate sexual abuse. It is *always* an irresponsible and destructive act of the adult who is the perpetrator. The child is always the innocent victim.

You will long for the days before these terrible memories surfaced. Though your former denial may look comfortable in retrospect, your memories were always present, though not necessarily conscious. Your mind had to work very hard at denial, continually taking a heavy emotional toll. Though unacknowledged by you, your memories were influencing your decisions and relationships in negative ways.

Facing the truth about the past will begin a long hard journey. However, you *are* on the road to healing! You will come to a time when you are not controlled by the abuse and your reactions to it. It takes great courage to face hard memories and work through them so they no longer have the power to run your life. It is vital not to do this alone, but with the help of a competent therapist.

Though God may seem far-off, uncaring, and perhaps even cruel for having let this happen, he will walk through this with you. *He* is not the Destroyer, he is the Healer. You may question his ways and means, but his action in your life will always be toward healing. Consider these words from James, "Behold, we count those blessed who endured. You have heard of the endurance of Job and have seen the outcome of the Lord's dealings, that the Lord is full of compassion and *is* merciful" (James 5:11). Joshua says, "Have I not commanded you? Be strong and courageous! Do not tremble or be dismayed, for the Lord your God is with you wherever you go" (Joshua 1:9).

NINE

I Was Raped—Life Will Never Be the Same

ANXIETY MARKED MARIA'S FACE when she first consulted me. "I'm having a very difficult time," she began. "I'm frightened by my feelings. About a month ago, leaving my job late at night, I was raped by a man on the janitorial staff. I'm still angry, anxious, and afraid. I can't concentrate on my work. Everyone was very sympathetic when the rape first occurred, but now they seem to think I should be over it 'after all this time.' Also, my husband is frustrated because we used to enjoy a good sex life, but I'm afraid to let go now. I don't sleep well and often have nightmares. Is something terribly wrong with me? The man who raped me was fired and I've brought charges against him. I feel like this will never be over."

What Maria was experiencing is known as post-traumatic stress disorder, a set of characteristic symptoms which can occur following any psychologically traumatic event, including rape. The precipitating event disrupts a person's ability to cope and causes a loss of psychological equilibrium for a time. Though each of us reacts to trauma in an individual way, certain feelings and behaviors occur in most people.

To help Maria, she and I first discussed what most women go through after a sexual assault. This enabled her and her husband to understand what she was experiencing, as well as to have some idea of what lay ahead as she progressed toward healing. I explained that the phase immediately following rape is by far the most intense and crucial. Though a woman may report a wide range of feelings, they usually are manifested in one of two ways. One is an unnaturally controlled response, where a woman appears calm and subdued, almost as if it didn't happen. The other is overtly expressive, where a woman clearly shows fear, anxiety, and anger through restlessness, crying, tension, or hysteria.

The intense and painful feelings that follow rape can cause great shifts in behavior. Activities that used to bring pleasure may no longer be enjoyable; people you once felt close to may now evoke feelings of estrangement. Even body movements may grow mechanical. Others may perceive the victim as withdrawn or daydreamy. She may have periods of uncontrolled crying, unable to handle her emotions. She may want to escape from life, and show little to no interest in work, home, or others. She may feel like going to bed and pulling up the covers (indeed, she may be wise to do exactly that for awhile!). Conversely, she may be terrified to be alone, even though she feels equally insecure when with others. In the end, she may have little or no contact with anyone.

Anxiety may become so great that the woman may be confused, unable to think clearly, indecisive, and lacking judgment. This helplessness causes her to believe she's lost control of her life. Feelings of guilt and shame may occur, sometimes intensified by the responses of others. Some women keep reliving the attack, going over every detail, wondering what they could have done to prevent it. Many experience recurring nightmares. Even distinguishing between the past and the present may be difficult. A woman may find herself lost in the past, especially if something suddenly triggers her memory. And of course there is the reaction of anger which may be expressed inappropriately.

Physically, a raped woman may become hyper-alert and jumpy. Nausea, a decreased appetite, bodily soreness, and frequently a diminished interest—even fear—of sex are not unusual. Difficult and extreme as these reactions are, I assured Maria, they *will* begin to subside once this first stage runs its course.

The second phase is readjustment. The victim knows she is beginning to readjust because slowly she is wanting to resume her daily routine. She is taking her focus off of her assault and concentrating on the aspects of her life which were neglected during the post-traumatic period. As she becomes less obsessed by thoughts of the attack she will feel great relief. Even though the nightmares may continue, and she may still startle easily, those negative reactions will become less intense, less painful. As her focus begins to shift from internal feelings to external events, she will become more and more active. She may have a renewed interest in sex at this point or it may yet be delayed. If a budding interest in sex is blotted out by anxiety or fear, that is natural and will pass.

Integration, the final stage, is when life and routine are back to normal. With emotions calmed down, it's a time to reflect on the attack to process whatever is still unresolved. Old feelings of guilt and anger may reappear at times, renewing your anger at the rapist. And because this is a time of introspection, she may again feel cut off from others to a degree. She may have some difficulty with nightmares, fears of being alone, or enjoying sex. If she is pressing charges, this phase may coincide with the trial, forcing her to relive the event and to ask herself if the rape will ever really be over.

But as she learns more and more how to integrate this experience into her life, the difficulties it has produced will begin to lessen, and then gradually disappear. "Though the process is long and difficult," I assured Maria, "it is not without hope."

What did Maria do to avoid getting bogged down in the

painful healing process? The quality and extent of the support she received from others was crucial. Those closest to her sometimes hindered and sometimes helped her. She needed to be reminded frequently that her reactions and thoughts were normal, and the reassurance helped her regain her self-confidence.

It was vital for her to talk to someone about the assault. Only by putting her thoughts and feelings into words could she get them into perspective and thus remove some of the nightmarish quality. Fortunately, those she talked with struck the right balance between respecting the pace of her progress and helping her move forward, without denying her experience.

Because those close to a victim respond subjectively, a competent counselor can better assure her the freedom to work through her problem. At the same time, finding a good counselor does not mean that support from those she loves and who love her is not still very significant. But as she begins to reconstruct her life, those dear ones may prematurely assume that everything is resolved and behind her.

Maria also needed to hear that the rape had caused problems for her husband. Though he was the one to whom she was closest and his responses were the most critical to her healing, he was angry and frightened by the assault, too. He worried that somehow he had failed to take care of her. He found her emotional and sexual distance difficult, and struggled not to take it personally. Because of the stress, he even became impatient at Maria's ups and downs. Due to the intensity of Maria's feelings, she had mistakenly assumed that she alone was suffering.

All those who are close to a rape victim will grapple with similar responses at various levels of intensity. That is especially true of a husband. He may need to be in counseling as well. Certainly he needs someone other than his wife with whom he can discuss his feelings.

If you have been the victim of rape, remember that the

impact of such an assault is deep. When you chastise your-self for falling short in your recovery, remind yourself of the severity of the experience. You may doubt your own ability, and that of your husband's, to deal with such a crisis. Though it may seem impossible at times, it is not so.

The prophet says in Lamentations 2:13; "For your ruin is as vast as the sea; who can heal you?" You may think that even God himself cannot reach the depths of your wound. But David says that he is the Lord "Who heals all your dis-eases; Who redeems your life from the pit; Who crowns you with lovingkindness and compassion; Who satisfies your years with good things, *so that* your youth is renewed like the eagle" (Psalm 103:3-5). These words do not promise instantaneous healing; rather, they promise that even in the darkness, when you feel desolate and alone, he is Lord, and he *will* redeem your life from the pit.

TEN

I Feel So Tired, But the Doctor Says, "Nothing Physical Is Wrong."

"I 'M TIRED ALL THE TIME. It doesn't matter how long I sleep, I'm more tired when I wake up than when I went to bed. I have friends who work, who take care of their homes and families, and even pursue extracurricular activities. I don't know how they do it! I don't work, my children are in school all day, and I can barely get out of bed in the morning! After I get the kids off to school, what do I do? I go back to bed and sleep a few more hours! What's the matter with me?"

Those words are typical of someone suffering from "chronic fatigue," one of the most frequent complaints brought to doctors today. The causes are diverse and only rarely related to excessive physical exertion. As a matter of fact, chronic fatigue is often a consequence of under-exertion rather than over-exertion.

Fatigue can be the result of overworking muscles so that carbon dioxide and lactic acid accumulate in the blood and drain the person of strength. Fatigue from this cause is usually of short duration and the cure is easy; rest and let the muscles restore themselves.

However, persistent weariness may also be a warning signal of an underlying physical problem, ranging from the flu to cancer. Anyone who feels exhausted for several weeks should have a thorough physical examination, including tests for diabetes, thyroid deficiency, and anemia.

A recent study, however, showed that a virus was not found in the throat or blood of people with the chronic fatigue syndrome. It is possible that several different viruses may be the causes of chronic fatigue, and many studies are pursuing that possibility. If medical research ends with only negative results, the conclusion usually is that the fatigue is psychological in origin.

Once a physical cause is ruled out, emotional difficulties or conflicts are considered by far the most common cause of prolonged tiredness. Sometimes fatigue can be an unconscious way to avoid facing unpleasant realities, such as the reasons behind depression or anxiety. We may be unhappy about our job, our marriage, or our place in life. Not dealt with, these difficulties may manifest themselves physically in fatigue. Perhaps "tired housewife syndrome" better describes mothers who face the same predictable routine, day in and day out, with no other adults to talk to and nothing to look forward to. Even if their physical activity is not excessive (though certainly chasing toddlers can be!), they are tired, depressed, and often resentful of their husband's involvement in the wider world. On the other hand, mothers working outside the home who feel guilty about leaving their children, are not only experiencing confusion about their roles, but also are experiencing *genuine* fatigue from trying to be "superwoman." Other examples are people bogged down in dull or overwhelming jobs. Still others are worn down by family conflicts.

Psychologically induced fatigue is often compounded by sleep irregularities. Whatever is troubling us interferes with restful sleep, and we awake more exhausted than when we went to bed. Women, whose schedules allow, deal with this by sleeping for long periods during the day. This results in even more guilt and depression when they look back at the end of the day and see that nothing productive has been accomplished.

If you have experienced any of these kinds of chronic fatigue, what can you do to find the cause of it? And what can you do to resolve whatever is causing it? First, you must get a thorough exam, to determine whether your fatigue has a physical origin. Having eliminated that, search your emotional state. Are your husband and children gone all day leaving you alone and lonely? Are you reasonably content in your marriage? If not, why not? Have you discussed your dissatisfactions with your husband, or kept them to yourself? Are you afraid to face what is missing in your life? Have you lost hope for change? Any major conflict or pervasive unhappiness when denied and buried, can result in the chronic fatigue we have been discussing.

What about your relationships with your children? Are you really involved in their lives? Or has your role been reduced to caretaker? Are you just performing motherly duties, without relating to the children themselves? Did you expect children to fill a void in your marriage, and are you disappointed that they didn't? What are your goals for them, your hopes for your relationships with them? Are you consciously involved in helping to shape their individual characters? On the other hand, are you so concerned about their growth and development that you are unable to have fun with them?

What about yourself? What are your interests outside of your children? What goals do you have for your own future? Is your life in a holding pattern, rather than a growing one? Are you able to maintain healthy relationships with friends? And finally, are you doing anything to stretch your mind? Are you taking time out for yourself?

I ask these questions, not for the purpose of pushing you in a particular direction, but rather to get you to examine some of the causes for your fatigue. Ask yourself questions like: What am I afraid of? What do I most want to avoid? Where do I feel most unhappy? What am I angry about? If I were not tired and could pursue anything I wanted, what would that be? Remember that chronic fatigue is usually a symptom of something we are having difficulty with and do not want to confront.

Meanwhile, there are some things you can do to alleviate this fatigue. Women who are chronically tired often do not eat well, so take a close look at your diet. If you use sugar and caffeine as quick pick-ups, you will find that they only pick you up for a moment, and then leave you lower than when you began. They do not give you a steady supply of blood sugar, but rather, a quick surge of energy that only results in deeper tiredness. Also, contrary to what you might think, exercise will increase your energy rather than decrease it. Regular exercise not only increases your body's ability to handle physical work, but also has a calming effect, draining off tension. Needless to say, sleep patterns improve when regular exercise becomes an integral part of your day.

In addition to taking these steps to improve your physical condition, it may be both wise and necessary to seek professional help. A counselor could help you discover internal conflicts and find constructive ways of resolving them. If you do not make the effort to face the difficulty and seek assistance in resolving it, your continued lethargy will only exacerbate your problems. The less you do, the more guilty you will feel, and the less you will feel capable of doing.

God has not called us to empty lives, but ones that are full. Don't settle for less.

Part Two

A Woman and Her Marriage

ELEVEN

Is It Okay for Christian Spouses to Disagree?

CONFLICT IS DIFFICULT FOR MANY PEOPLE. Couples who do not know how to handle disagreements in their marriage often have the mistaken notion that unity means never disagreeing. The result is that one spouse tends to remain silent to preserve an outward appearance of unity. The outcome of this passivity, however, is buried anger and bitterness, which silently erode the marriage. Is it wrong for Christian spouses to disagree? And if it is not, is there a good way to handle the conflict?

All human beings, even those who share a love of God, do differ. Anybody who has served on a church committee or been responsible for overseeing a church function, or developed a Christian friendship knows this is so. We preach love, yet we disagree, sometimes bitterly. We talk about bearing with one another, yet show intolerance. We preach humility, but we are often sure we are right. The result is an outward harmony which is really only a pretense. The quarrel is driven underground. Above ground, or near the surface, are criticism, resentment, and bitterness.

All Christians are called to unity, and we are certainly to strive for it in our marriages. Paul says, "Being diligent to preserve the unity of the Spirit in the bond of peace"

(Ephesians 4:3); and "Make my joy complete by being of the same mind, maintaining the same love, united in spirit, intent on one purpose" (Philippians 2:2). But what does that mean in a marriage? Must you and your husband agree about everything? If so, there obviously is a problem.

It is a given that two imperfect human beings—with different personalities, different backgrounds, varying needs, and levels of maturity—will not be echoes of one another. Paul himself experienced this. When he was first converted (Acts 9), the genuineness of the change was questioned because of his previous attitude toward Christians. Barnabas intervened and smoothed the way for his acceptance by the other apostles. These two men then traveled and ministered together with extraordinary results. And then they disagreed—and it was a sharp disagreement—with no bending on either side. The quarrel was not over a doctrinal truth, but over a third companion. The result was that they separated.

I do not use this example as a model for handling disagreement. Rather, it illustrates that conflict is to be expected, and it is common to life. Even Jesus disagreed with many people! The question, then, is not "Is disagreement acceptable?" Instead, the question is, "*How* should Christians handle disagreement?"

The first step is to react with caution. Argument fuels anger, hurt, and fear—emotions that pump up the adrenaline and cause us to behave impulsively. Proverbs is filled with admonitions to use caution: "The heart of the righteous ponders how to answer, but the mouth of the wicked pours out evil things" (15:28), "He who restrains his words has knowledge, and he who has a cool spirit is a man of understanding" (17:27), "Do not go out hastily to argue your case; otherwise, what will you do in the end when your neighbor puts you to shame?" (25:8), and "When there are many words, transgression is unavoidable, but he who restrains his lips is wise" (10:19).

We are told in Jeremiah 17:9, "The heart is more deceitful than all else and is desperately sick; who can understand it?" If this is true, caution is more than warranted! How often we legitimize our response by declaring, "I'm saying this for your own good!" Are we really saying it out of concern for the other—or for ourselves? More likely, we did not like what they did, we are hurt or angry, we want things our way, or—puppet-like—we're mouthing phrases we heard in our childhood homes. If our hearts are truly deceitful, then we need to exercise caution until we have first examined our hearts.

We would do well before we respond verbally to pause and ask ourselves some questions. With what do I disagree? What are the possible ways of handling this disagreement? What would be my reasons for choosing any of these ways? What results do I hope to achieve? What needs am I trying to meet in myself? Let's consider each of these questions separately.

First, with what do I disagree? This may seem like a foolish question, but so often arguments end up being about everything except the original disagreement. In the midst of our hurt and anger we dredge up the past and start flinging around statements that begin with "You always…" or "You never…" Pause to clarify the focus of your disagreement. The more clearly we can formulate it, the more easily we will be able to stay on the central point even when emotion mounts. We will also have more success in getting our spouse to understand exactly what we mean if we can state it clearly to ourselves. This process prevents our being led into a disagreement on sheer emotion. Perhaps the actual disagreement is not over the content of what was said, but stems, rather, from an emotion stirred up by a look, a tone of voice, or reminder of an old memory.

The second question regarding ways of handling this disagreement, will force us to be more creative. Most of us have a particular style—often simply what we saw our parents do. Perhaps silence was a shield our parents used; maybe one parent was highly volatile and another feared confrontation. We tend to use these methods over and over again, without thinking through other possibilities.

Certainly one way of responding to minor conflict is silence. If a man and woman disagree about every little thing, their words become petty and ridiculous. Silence is the correct response when the issue is insignificant, or the time is not right for airing it. Or perhaps you have been going around in circles and it would be wiser to find a mediator to help. Or you may be still unclear regarding your own position. In these instances silence might indeed be the better course. But silence should *not* be chosen because you are afraid to confront, because you think you should never have disagreements, because you are using silence as punishment, or because that is what a parent modeled.

Another solution is to ask questions. Often we really have not understood the other point of view. Proverbs 18:13 says, "He who gives an answer before he hears, It is folly and shame to him." We need to be sure we have heard the other person correctly, which means we have not only heard but *understood* what he meant. It is amazing how often our emotions, fears, and personal history make us hear incorrectly.

One couple I worked with illustrates this very well. The man kept reiterating that all he wanted was just for her to love him. Sounds fine, right? She said she just needed a little space every once in awhile. Sounds reasonable, right? As we probed these seemingly right requests in counseling, we found that he meant that he wanted her "in his back pocket" *all* the time. That was what love meant. She defined space as being able to do whatever she wanted, whenever she felt like it. The argument was intense and never came to resolution because each assumed they knew what the other meant. Acceptable words camouflaged unacceptable expectations.

Stating our opinions and ideas is an option we need to use without attacking our spouse. The purpose of a rejoinder is not so much to make the other person see it our way, but to share new thoughts so that a solution that considers both views might be found. The word confront comes from Latin and literally means, "together forehead." Other meanings are "to put together," "to construct," "to compose," and "to invent." These convey very different meanings than the common one of convincing others to do things the "right" way—i.e., our way! These definitions imply creativity—the creation of a way that expressly takes into account the needs and ideas of two people.

"What are the motives directing my choice?" is another way of asking, "Is there deceitfulness in my heart?" Am I speaking because I cannot tolerate a difference of opinion? Am I choosing silence simply because that is what I am comfortable with? Am I selecting a response to pay back for the hurt I am feeling? If any of these are so, then the message will not be that I want to work out the disagreement, but that I am out to take care of myself. Rather than resolving the disagreement, it will probably be intensified.

Fourth, what results do I hope to achieve? Am I aiming for peace at any price? Is my goal to get my way? Am I intent on changing my spouse, or am I truly considering his good? Am I actively looking for constructive ways to disagree which will lead to our personal growth as well as a solution? Weaving together each person's input and ideas may bring an unexpected, innovative solution—one that may not suit other couples, but is uniquely suited to both of you.

Lastly, what needs am I trying to meet within myself? Do I need to resolve disagreements so that I feel important? Do I need to "win"? Do I just use arguments to rid myself of anger and hurt? What is the force that pushes me on to disagree?

Paul talks about what should push us in 2 Corinthians 5:14 where he says, "For the love of Christ constrains us..." (Philips). The word constrain means to force or drive. The driving force behind everything we do should be the love of Christ. We are not to resolve disagreements just because we are uncomfortable with them, or because we feel hurt, afraid, or angry. Nor are we are to resolve them with silence just to get someone to leave us alone, or because we feel inadequate to speak. We must disagree in a way that is motivated by the love of Christ. Our disagreements should be governed by what we are taught in 1 Corinthians 13 and Philippians 2. These teachings will help us determine whether to be silent or to speak. They will also help set our tone of voice, our timing, our choice of words.

God gave you to your mate to help him, to sharpen him, to encourage him, and to *add* to him. An echo, which is in effect silence, can do none of these things.

Disagreement does not necessarily mean a lack of unity, but it can result in disunity when handled divisively, selfishly. Disagreement that is driven by the love of Christ can sharpen us as individuals and at the same time help us achieve true unity and harmony in our marriage.

God could have made us all alike, but he chose not to. If we learn to handle our disagreements well, they can bring about much-needed change, a new way of looking at something, a softening of an attitude—all hallmarks of growth. Do not seek superficial, meaningless unity with your spouse. Instead pursue the true unity that is born of mutual understanding and caring. When you disagree, be compelled by the love of Christ, seeking not your personal good, but the good of both. Your marriage cannot help but be enriched.

TWELVE

I've Never Found Sex Satisfying

MANY WOMEN COME TO ME FOR HELP with various sexual difficulties. By far, the most common is inability to achieve orgasm. It is sad when women struggle in silence, because help is available. But first, let's consider sex in its God-given context.

Sex is God's invention. He thought it up, and all that he created, he declared good. It's sad that many Christian women do not believe this. At worst they see sex as dirty and sinful, and at best, a duty to be endured. Both are a far cry from God's intent. Not only did God invent sex, he intended it to be pleasurable for *both* men and women. No place in Scripture even hints that women should not be interested in sex, or enjoy it. In Song of Songs both man and woman actively participate in, and take delight in, their sexual union.

These poetically beautiful passages contradict the idea that society, both secular and Christian, too often has taught—that the woman is to be passive sexually. Because women who are confident and assertive in the sexual relationship are often considered a threat to men, many of us have schooled ourselves in restraint. Unfortunately, in doing that we have deprived both ourselves and our husbands of a fuller, richer experience. The woman in Song of Songs is neither passive or dependent!

Female anatomy is obviously different from male anatomy, but that does not in any way mean that the woman is the more passive. When a woman assumes the passive role she usually has the mistaken idea that her husband is the sexual expert, and that her orgasm is his responsibility. In reality, a satisfying sexual experience is mutual and requires two active partners. Both need to approach lovemaking with the belief that sex is good. Both need to approach it with a sense of freedom.

Orgasm is more than physical. The psychological element is very much involved as well. Orgasmic women are usually confident enough to initiate sex and able to express their needs and preferences. They are actively involved in the experience, both physically and psychologically. Clearly, these qualities are more likely to be present in a healthy marriage that is based on trust. When a woman does not trust her husband, her confidence, expressiveness, and initiative are diminished.

What can you and your husband do to improve your sexual relationship? First, do not forget that sex is just one way of expressing your love of each other; current books, magazines, and media send messages to the contrary. Sex is a unique and wonderful way of relating, one that is meant to provide an oasis for both man and woman, but it is not the only way. Every marriage includes areas of loving that require more effort than others. Try not to let difficulties with sex deprive you of other marital joys. Though frustration is understandable, you have reason to expect success. Try to transfer some of the confidence derived from other aspects of your marriage into the sexual arena. Why should you have joy in other areas of your life together and not this one?

Orgasm alone does not define a good sexual experience. A sexual relationship should be seen in the context of the marriage as a whole. A sexual coming together can be good, even pleasurable, without orgasm. While frustration with the lack of orgasm is understandable, it is important not to let that overshadow what you have that is good. Do not throw the whole of your sexual relationship out the window for lack of an orgasm, or you will have reduced it to nothing more than a reflex response, and sex between a husband and wife is far greater than that! To conclude that sex is not good at all, simply for lack of an orgasm, is to fail to understand sex as God intended it. Yes, he intended physical pleasure. However, physical release alone does not necessarily mean the sexual relationship is good. Nor does the lack of an orgasm mean that a sexual relationship is a failure.

Keeping these things in mind, let's look at some specific steps you and your husband might take to increase your sexual responsiveness. First, set aside a length of time during which you both agree not to have intercourse. During this time, cut back on outside commitments. What you are going to do is go "incrementally," from an initial sexual relationship to its culmination in intercourse.

Begin as if you were brand new lovers—taking every opportunity to touch each other in affectionate ways. Lightly stroke a shoulder, a face. Hold hands. Nothing more. After a few days add hugging, then kissing. Take your time and enjoy! After a few more days, move to caressing each other's bodies, except for the genital areas. Do this first with clothes on, then without.

During this time talking is very important. Let each other know what pleases and what does not. These are to be relaxed times, away from the pressures of children and outsiders. No television, no phone, and no deadlines! Nothing and nobody should be allowed to interfere. When this has become a relaxed and enjoyable time for both of you, include touching the genital areas, but still with no concern for orgasm. All you are doing is enjoying the sexual feelings and continuing to talk about what you like and what you don't. When you both feel ready, add *manual* stimulation to reach orgasm. It will be vital to continue sharing what is pleasurable at this point. Once you have achieved orgasm with some degree of success, then intercourse becomes a natural continuation of your lovemaking.

One of the great benefits of this method is that each of you will become very aware of what pleases the other. Many couples spend their entire married life ignorant of what gives sexual pleasure to one another. They just guess and assume they are right. You will also learn to enjoy simply being sexual, with or without orgasm. The freedom to do this will greatly enrich your sex life together.

If you follow these steps carefully, and are still left dissatisfied, I suggest that you see a qualified therapist together. Your personal histories, fears, or attitudes may need to be explored. But do not give up. God has provided this pleasure for your mutual benefit. Continue to love, encourage, and support one another, with the realization that just as your oneness in other areas has developed, so it can in this area as well. Actively pursue loving each other without shyness or fear. Eventually each of you will be able to say of the other, "May he kiss me with the kisses of his mouth! For your love is better than wine. His mouth is full of sweetness. And he is wholly desirable. This is my beloved and this is my friend, O daughter of Jerusalem" (Song of Songs 1:2; 5:16).

THIRTEEN

How Can I Survive the Pain of His Adultery?

H OW DOES A WOMAN OVERCOME the most shattering thing that can happen to a marriage, the one thing that threatens to irrevocably destroy the most sacred bond between two people?

After years of what Edna believed was a strong relationship and good family life, she has discovered Bob has had an ongoing relationship with another woman. He says the affair is over, and asks for forgiveness. She wants to believe him, but has lost confidence in her ability to truly know and trust him, not having even suspected his infidelity. Wanting to hold on to her marriage, and, at the same time, not wanting to continue what she sees as a dishonest relationship, she feels stuck—and afraid. Can she ever forget it happened? Can she ever get over the pain? Can she ever trust Bob again?

Adultery is a terrible tear in the fabric of a marriage, but it is not necessarily the end of the tapestry that two people are weaving together. If Edna and Bob are to recover from the brokenness both now feel, there are several things which they must understand.

The first thing is that, emotionally, each is in a very different place. Edna is reeling from *brand new* knowledge that is shocking and incredulous. Perhaps she is still in denial, insisting it is all a bad dream. Bob, on the other hand, has *known* what he was doing for a long time. He is not in shock. He knows perfectly well that it is *not* a dream, but a reality with which he has been living. In addition, he's probably carrying great guilt.

Because Edna and Bob are starting from different places, with different feelings, it is very natural for them to misjudge each other. Edna *needs* to ask questions to understand what has happened. Bob wants only to *forget*. Unlike his wife, he is at the place of wanting her to forgive him, so the two of them can move on from here.

This great difference in perspective can cause many problems unless Bob and Edna both understand that it exists. Edna, for example, might think Bob is trying to minimize her reactions or wants her to take forgiveness lightly, but this may not be so. Bob's frustration may cause him to say things like, "Well, why don't you just forgive me so we can put this behind us?" Edna's need to continue questioning him fuels his guilt, so he resists answering. All of this can cause even greater distance between them. Therefore, Bob and Edna will be wise to find an objective third party to help them work out the reconciliation process.

If you find yourself in similar circumstances, what can you expect to lie ahead? Once the shock and disbelief begin to wear off, anger usually follows. Anger toward your husband, expressed in angry questions. How did I fail him? What does she have that I don't? How could he have betrayed me? He couldn't love me! You will need guidance to curb the human impulse to return the hurt. Though an understandable reaction, striking back will only cause further damage to your marriage.

As the reality of your situation sinks in, you will feel much grief. You have lost something precious to you, something you trusted was there. Any loss is a kind of death, and so you must grieve. But try to remember that this loss is not the same as a greater loss, the death of your marriage. It is not even the end of a good, solid marriage based on trust, but the loss of your marriage *as you assumed it to be*. It will be important to keep in mind that the God whom you worship is constantly bringing new life out of death. Unlike you, he is not limited by the failings of your marriage, and therefore he is able to bring life out of the death that has come. Grieve for what is gone, but continue to hope in God for a new understanding and a new basis for the more mature relationship that is to come.

While you are experiencing all of these reactions, your husband will be grappling with his own turmoil. Whatever beliefs he has had previously about his trustworthiness have been shattered. This will make it painful for him to hear about your fears and your inability to trust him now which is one reason he will keep urging you to move on and forget the past.

Both of you have seen, from opposite ends of the continuum, that God's word is indeed true when it says, "The heart is more deceitful than all else and is desperately sick; who can understand it?" (Jeremiah 17:9). Your husband will have to struggle with his failure to be who he thought he was, who he wants to be, and indeed, who he promised you he would be. This will produce in him a second response similar to yours, one of great grief. Not only will he grieve for what has happened to your marriage, but he will also mourn the loss of a positive self-image.

Just as both of you need to remind one another that God brings life out of death, so you also need to remember that *all* of our hearts are equally deceitful. It might be easy for both of you to focus on your husband's actions and point to him as the one with the deceptive heart, but God's word speaks of *all* hearts. Part of the healing process will be an ever-growing awareness, and acceptance, of how you have each hurt your marriage. This is not in any way to justify your husband's adultery, for he has sinned against you in a terrible way. Nor is it to say that you are in any way responsible for his wrong choice. It is said to help you avoid falling into the trap of simply dissecting your husband and his sin. To allow the wrong done by others to become our focus only hinders our own growth.

As you can see, your individual reactions may easily cause further wounds, because your needs and responses will more than likely be out of step with each other. The insight and wisdom of a third party can help you prevent that possibility.

While you both are working on internal struggles, give attention to the external as well. You might try to establish some pleasant activities and time together. What sort of things have you enjoyed in the past? What did you like about those activities? What could you do now to reestablish some of those happy times? Or perhaps plan new ones that incorporate the aspects you found enjoyable. Some things you did before you would find painful right now. Save them for later. But, on the other hand, were good times alone together lost in the shuffle of responsibility for children, home, and jobs? Reintroduce them now. Even better, you may come up with new ideas, fun things with no history attached to them.

At any rate, as hard as it seems, and as much as you may not want to do so right now, reestablishing enjoyable shared experiences is crucial. Otherwise, your relationship will consist of nothing but painful problems. While you are "dating," agree to take a break from talking about the affair and other concerns.

Both of you will need to talk with someone, besides with each other, about the affair. You will want to ask: What was your husband looking for? Why did he choose to look outside the marriage? Were there ways in which you unwittingly made it difficult for him to find these things with you? Explore, too, your expectations of each other and your marriage. Were they realistic? What did your marriage not provide? No marriage can fill all needs, so how else can they be met? Finally, is it true that *all* our needs *have* to be fulfilled, as our society suggests?

Woven throughout the healing process is learning the art of forgiveness. Have you grasped the truth of God's forgiveness, which is "If we confess our sins, he is faithful and righteous to forgive us our sins and to cleanse us from all unrighteousness" (1 John 1:9)? Though your husband obviously requires your forgiveness, you will likely discover you also require his.

This kind of forgiveness is not possible for humans to achieve alone, because it is based on a true understanding of every person's need of God's forgiveness. As you steep yourself in an acceptance of God's love and forgiveness for yourself, you will be able to draw out of that deep well the ability to forgive your husband. Forgiveness does *not* mean that you will never remember what has happened. To forget would be foolish, if not impossible. You need to remember that it happened so that you can work more carefully together in the future. It *does* mean that you do not remind one another of past sins, but instead keep your sights on the love and forgiveness of God. It also means that you do not repay evil for evil, but rather good for evil, as did the One whom you follow.

Finally, you will likely need to work on your sexual relationship. You may feel especially vulnerable and want very much to close down. If so, I would urge you to start slowly. Learn to be comfortable together sexually again, which may mean starting with just sitting together on the sofa while you watch a movie. As you begin to feel more relaxed with each other, your sexual desire will likely return. Here again, a third party might be helpful, especially if sexual problems existed before the affair. If that is true, the temptation may be not to discuss them now, for fear of intensifying feelings of inadequacy and guilt. However, that is all the more reason to talk about them. If they are ignored, they will continue to undermine your marriage, and help set you up for future failure.

Since marriage is a lifelong commitment, it is always in process. Some seasons of a marriage are good and fruitful; others seem barren, painful, and difficult. The marriage relationship encompasses all these things and more, but it is never reduced to any one of them. Do not think that your marriage is over. Do not assume it can never be as good as it was. It is true that it can never be the same as it was, but by God's grace, it can be richer and fuller than you ever imagined it to be. God is able "Now to Him who is able to do exceeding abundantly beyond all that we ask or think, according to the power that works within us" (Ephesians 3:20). He will do that in your heart, as he changes and teaches you. He will do that in your husband's heart. Trust that he will do that in your marriage. Try to persevere in the difficult work that lies ahead, and trust God to bring life out of the death you are facing.

FOURTEEN

My Husband Is Abusive— What Should I Do?

C ORRIE CAME INTO MY OFFICE not too long ago with the following story:

"I have a very difficult problem which I've never discussed with anyone. My husband and I have been married
twelve years and we have four children. He has an important position in our denomination. Everyone likes him and
thinks he's doing a great job. Often he's asked to do public
speaking.

"The problem is that my husband often beats me and the
children. He gets very angry when we don't act the way he
thinks we should. He started hitting me just after we were
married—he only did it once before we were married. I've
never told a soul, partly because I'm afraid of him, but also
because he's a prominent figure in our church and I don't
think anyone would believe me. I love my husband, but the
abuse is getting worse, and I don't know what to do."

The undeniable fact that violence occurs in seemingly
happy Christian homes is so disturbing that many simply
refuse to believe that it is possible. Unfortunately, statistics
indicate otherwise. Violence is not limited to the poor, un-
educated, or irreligious. It is also found among the wealthy

and educated, as well as the so-called conservative religious right.

Who are these battered women? Again, the stereotypes do not fit. Women who are abused do not necessarily come from abusive homes, they are not masochistic, nor do they come from a particular ethnic group or class. It is true, however, that many do come from traditional homes where sex-role stereotyping was strong. They grew up with the expectation that they would marry a man who would care for them as their father had. Dependency on a man is usually a factor. These women usually have a strong commitment to a patriarchal ideology as well as to the institution of marriage.

An abused woman develops what is called "learned helplessness." This means that when she is caught in a situation where repeated attempts to bring about change fail, she learns to be helpless. For example, a wife may continually work to please her husband in the way she keeps house. When her efforts fail, she may become passive, listless, and give up all hope of change. In other words, when a woman believes she can do nothing to control her situation after many tries to do so, she will act helpless. Her failure to see herself as an influential force usually leads to anxiety and depression.

The violence in abusive homes seems to occur in a cyclical manner with three phases. First there is the buildup of tension, then the explosion, and finally the contrition when the abuser becomes sorry and loving.

During the first phase minor abuses occur, frequently verbal ones. The woman at this point believes that she still has some control; that if only she will do the right thing she can prevent the abuse. She clings to the belief that if the house is clean, if the dinner is cooked correctly, and if the children behave, her husband will not get angry. In her efforts to control her husband she becomes very compliant, and if he does not become angry, she feels she has succeeded. If, however, he explodes, then obviously she has failed in some way. In this manner she takes on the responsibility for her husband's abusive behavior. She denies the anger that she feels, and instead she excuses and justifies his behavior since she believes she is the cause of it. His aggressiveness increases in proportion to her passivity, and the tension between them escalates.

The second phase is the actual battering. Obviously a woman's anticipation of the inevitable abuse causes her great stress. She may lose sleep, eat irregularly, and have severe headaches or other physical symptoms. Sometimes the waiting becomes so unbearable that she will act in such a way as to force her husband's hand. Since the abuse is inevitable, she reasons, they may as well get it over with. She is *not* indicating that she likes the role of the battered wife. She just feels the battering is inevitable. She has also discovered that a constant state of fear and threat is often worse than the actual violence. By provoking the attack she is resorting to the only vestige of control she has.

Once the attack is over, the third phase begins. It is characterized by loving, pleading, and contrite behavior on the part of the batterer. It usually includes begging for forgiveness, and promising never to do such a thing again. This is followed by a period of calm when the abusing spouse becomes optimistic about himself. He now believes he can control himself and that his wife will never do anything to irritate him again. His wife responds by accepting that the behavior she sees in phase three represents the "real man." She feels he needs her, and she knows he needs help. If she leaves now he will never get the help that is so necessary, so she stays for his sake, and also in order to hold the family together. And so the cycle is repeated.

Unlike the women who are battered, most abusive men come from homes where abuse was present and usually from families who coped with anger and stress in unacceptable ways. Such men are often basically dependent, possessive, and lacking in ego strength. They can be intensely jealous and resort to constant surveillance of the wife's activities. Paul Tournier, in his book *The Violence Within*, said it this way: "Violence is a way of proving that one exists, when one believes oneself to be insignificant."

Abusive men seem to have dual personalities; they are friendly and happy in public, violent and mean in private. They appear to the world to be competent and strongly oriented toward family, but often they lie about their own behavior and that of their wives, blaming them for any problems. Charming and seductive when they get what they want, they turn violent and cruel when their desires are thwarted.

How can anyone break this cycle? Corrie has been caught in the cycle of abuse since before her marriage. What can be done to stop her husband's battering?

First, like Corrie, if you are in an abusive relationship you must recognize that you do not deserve the abuse. Every woman has been less than a perfect wife. All of us, in some way, fail those we love. Since we are not perfect, we can never completely meet the needs of another person, no matter how much we try. But *no* failure gives anyone the right to abuse, or makes any of us deserving of abuse.

Second, you are *not* responsible for your husband's behavior. He, and only he, is responsible for how he treats you and your children, regardless of anything you do or fail to do. You are not to blame.

Third, there is no virtue in suffering in silence. Proverbs 31:8-9 says: "Open your mouth for the dumb, for the rights of all the unfortunate. Open your mouth, judge righteously, and defend the rights of the afflicted and needy." In this case, the afflicted and needy are you and your children. You *must* seek help for yourself and for them. However, it is very important that you do not go to someone who will be so threatened by this information that they will refuse to believe you. If your husband is a public figure, as Corrie's

was, there will be people who will have a strong, if unconscious interest in your story being untrue. Choose a pastor, a
counselor, or a women's shelter where you will be believed
and protected. You will need support, insight, and practical
help for what lies ahead.

What can you expect? Change is not likely to occur unless
you take some action. Men who are abusers are so skilled at
blaming others for their own behavior that they deceive
even themselves. The idea that they need to change does not
occur to them. To effect change, even reconciliation, the first
step is the decision to leave, press assault charges, and refuse
to return to the marriage until your husband has completed
a counseling program for offenders. It is ironic that in order
to save your marriage you must disrupt it. Such a step will
require tremendous courage on your part and your husband
will blame you for the overwhelming consequences that will
follow. You must remember that striving to bring an end to
the abuse is an act of love for yourself, your children, and
even for your husband. What he is doing is sin—that needs
to be brought to light and confronted, so he can have the
opportunity to truly change.

It is vital for you to realize and accept at this point that
you have no control over the choice your husband makes.
This can be very frightening. Furthermore, you are not
responsible for whether he chooses reconciliation. Any
change that comes about in his heart, any true desire to learn
to obey God in his relationship with you, will be a direct
result of the grace of God. You cannot make this change happen, nor are you at fault if it doesn't.

Once you have confronted the situation, much that has
been submerged through the years will begin to surface. You
will be faced with your own anger and fear. You may find
yourself wishing for revenge. Grappling with these feelings
will take time and the support of a good counselor or
women's group.

Your husband, in the meantime, will be faced with a herculean task. He will have to look unflinchingly at his heinous actions and cope with the guilt that will inevitably follow. Confession, both private and public, will be necessary. Then he will need much help and support to unlearn old patterns and learn new ones. You will want to take your husband back, but it is crucial that you do not reunite with him prematurely. Learning new behaviors is very difficult. They will be fragile for a long time. Your presence and that of your children on a daily basis would put tremendous pressure on those frail, positive new patterns which he is learning. His healing will be long and hard, and there is no guarantee that he will respond as you might hope. Courage and perseverance will be necessary.

As Christians, we are called to fight against violence and cruelty wherever we find it. For you, that is in your own home. Of the many difficulties, your most difficult will be the possibility that you are breaking up your own home. Your husband will most likely encourage that concern, and perhaps others will also. A clear teaching of Scripture is that we are not to condone sin; we are not to make it easy or comfortable for another to sin. It will require tremendous courage to take a stand for righteousness and justice in your own home, seemingly "against" your own husband. Keep in mind that alignment with God's standards is always for, not against, another. To excuse sin, to strip another of his rightful responsibility, is to weaken him.

It was a long, hard road, but Corrie learned to take a stand for justice for herself and her children. She learned eventually to do so without vengeance or bitterness. She was able, after much hard work and support, to have the courage to "walk in her house in the integrity of her heart" (Psalm 101:2b).

FIFTEEN

My Husband Is Divorcing Me!

D IVORCE IS PAINFUL—very painful. It raises difficult questions and feelings, tears apart the fabric of many lives, and also has emotional, financial, and physical repercussions. Feelings of low self-esteem, guilt, depression, and anxiety must be struggled with. Those who set out on a course for divorce rarely realize the full ramifications of their decision. Life post-divorce is almost always more complicated than they expected.

There is no experience like divorce in a family's life. It is unique. Though there are similarities with those families who experience a death—since divorce is the death of a marriage—there are also vast differences. Divorce involves a choice, as well as a changed but continuing relationship between both parties. The resultant questions and struggles may continue for years.

I recently counseled a woman whose husband walked out the door after twelve years of marriage. She had two children under the age of eight. Their marriage had been a difficult one, but she thought it was bearable. Her husband simply said to her, "I want better than this."

If you find yourself in this situation, you will, like her, probably be reeling from shock. You began marriage full of love and hope. Whatever the difficulties you encountered, you have probably continued to hope that things would work out for the better. As the prospect of the divorce grows nearer, you may feel anger, resentment, guilt, fear, and loneliness. You may respond by withdrawing from life, or you may feel the need to talk. The sense of disbelief, the feeling that this cannot be happening to you, will continue for awhile. Until it passes, you will be only a passive player in the drama between you and your husband.

Once you face what is happening, you will move into a second stage—that of adjusting to a new reality. You will experience depression as you grieve for that which has been lost. You will question yourself regarding whose "fault" it is. You will struggle with guilt when you are convinced it is your fault. You will wrestle with intense anger, especially when you are convinced that the fault is his. There may be times of extreme loneliness for male companionship, as well as for a second parent in the home if there are children. You will end up handling responsibilities that are new to you—things your husband usually took care of. Holidays especially may emphasize your loss because family traditions are being continued without a primary member. There may also be the loss of some friendships, as well as a significant altering of your relationship with your in-laws.

But after a while, as you begin to pick up the pieces and learn to live life without your husband, you will enter a new stage—that of personal growth. You will begin to feel more control over your life. You will find you want to interact with other people, male and female. Now more hopeful about your future, you will become more competent, and able to reach new goals you may have set for yourself. You will have arrived at a routine with your children that makes you feel more adequate in handling them.

Your children will be going through stages not unlike yours. Their questions and feelings will probably be different because they are, after all, younger. They may assume the blame for the divorce. This may seem like an irrational reaction, but it is very common in children who have experienced the loss of a parent, whether through divorce or death. This assumption, although erroneous, is real, and children must be allowed to express it so it can be dealt with and put to rest. If his father leaves, a son may feel the split more intensely than a daughter, because boys identify more strongly with their fathers. You may see the effect in your daughter later in her life, particularly when she begins dating. Both may react by regressing developmentally. They may have trouble in school or with peers. Physical symptoms, such as stomach ailments, may appear, often because of an unconscious desire to stay close to home. Like you, they will feel out of control of their lives. Many of their reactions will be innocent and misguided attempts to regain some sense of control.

What can you do, while you and your children undergo these various changes, to handle them constructively? One very important step will be to find some good solid support for all of you. If you have not already done so, you should sit down with your pastor and tell him of your situation. Not only will you need his affirmation, but he may be able to suggest other people who could provide emotional support for you as well as for your children. You, as a single parent, will hardly be able to provide all the emotional sustenance that your youngsters will need, so it will be important for them to have someone else they can easily talk with. It is also crucial for you to have an outside "ear," so you will not fall into the trap of sharing unwisely with your children or leaning on them in ways that are not good for all of you as a family.

You will also need legal counsel. Many women end up financial victims of divorce. Though changes have been made in our legal system, women are still very vulnerable, particularly if they are not established in a job. When a divorce is bitter, money can become a powerful way to punish, thus wise and prompt legal counsel is mandatory.

I also hope you will find family and friends to be a tremendous help during your struggles, though there may be some who cannot accept the reality of your divorce and will unfortunately deal with it by detaching and "divorcing" you! This can be especially difficult to handle if they try to excuse their distance with phrases like, "I do not agree with what you are doing because I do not think it is scriptural. Therefore I cannot help." Hopefully, whether they understand and agree or not, you will have friends who will "be there" in a loving, non-judgmental, and Christ-like way. Even if they think you and your husband are wrong, it would be much more helpful if they have the wisdom to demonstrate love and forgiveness, rather than judgment.

A second important aspect is the manner in which you and your husband manage the children. Both of you need to avoid putting them in the middle and hurting them unnecessarily. Keep in mind that you cannot be both parents to your children. You can only be the parent that you are. Also, it is unwise to criticize your spouse in front of them, and it is important not to ask them to report on their father. As much as possible, you and your husband need to unite your efforts to maintain the children's usual routine. It is destructive to your children if you begin to turn to them for your emotional support or if you begin to maneuver their schedules in an attempt to keep them from their father. Try very hard to enable your children to retain some good memories of your marriage, difficult as it may be when you are feeling angry at their father and wishing for revenge. To hear your kids recall good memories of their dad may bring up the desire to contradict them with "If you only knew..." But those memories are very important to your children's well-being, and you need to give them the freedom to hold onto them.

A third thing to keep in mind is an understanding of the grieving process. You will experience times of depression and apathy. You may fear that life will never look hopeful again, or that you will not be able to manage for yourself and your children. There will be days when the emotional pain will cause you to want to hide under the covers and never come out. Some women often add to their anxieties by feeling that they have to push themselves to get up and do, as if nothing traumatic were going on in their lives. Rather than force activity on yourself, simplify your life during this time. When you are faced with a great deal of internal struggle and pain, it makes good sense to keep external demands to a minimum. The emotional reserves that you are used to having may feel depleted while you are dealing with so much going on inside you. If you are unable to cope, that is no reason for shame. It is a normal reaction during times of stress. Simplifying your life right now will help you handle your essential responsibilities in a better fashion.

Divorce is an attack on the family at its core. The reverberations will be felt by all of you for some time, and support from the body of Christ will be very important. You will need courage to face a painful reality, and wisdom for making decisions that will affect the future of both you and your children. You will need patience to walk through the various stages, knowing that each is temporary, and that God is with you in them all.

I have painted a painful picture, but, I think, a realistic one. There is no easy way to break up a marriage. However, God brings order out of chaos, light out of darkness, life out of death. At times, all you will see and feel will be chaos, darkness, and death. Moving unseen, however, will be the Giver of all life, working to bring healing and newness. As much as possible, surround yourself with those who will remind you of that. Find your support among those who will encourage you to stand firm, to learn to forgive, and to wait until God brings new life to you and your children.

As you walk forward, cling to the words of Isaiah: "You

whom I have taken from the ends of the earth, And called from its remotest parts, And said to you, 'You are my servant, I have chosen you and not rejected you. Do not fear for I am with you; do not anxiously look about you, for I am your God. I will strengthen you, surely I will help you, Surely I will uphold you with My righteous right hand'" (Isaiah 41:9-10).

SIXTEEN

I Feel Crippled Since My Husband's Death

S ARAH WAS TOTALLY OVERWHELMED by grief when her husband died. Having no energy for life or interest in people, she felt like a cripple. Even knowing that her husband
was a believer, and that he was with the Lord, she had questions about God and life that she had never considered
before. Unable to find peace anywhere, she didn't feel comfortable talking about her questions with others, particularly
those thoughts concerning God, for fear of being judged.

Few losses change an adult's life like that of a spouse's
death. After years of emotional and physical oneness, the
weaving together of two lives is suddenly severed and
threatens the one remaining. Life seems to have stopped and
emptiness seems to stretch ahead endlessly. No woman
could live as one flesh with a man for years, and not have his
death cause a deep wound. That wound will eventually
heal, but the process will take time, and the grief that follows
such a loss will be tremendous.

Grief is healthy. Too often Christians think they need to
hide their grief, as if it were wrong, or a sign of weakness or
lack of faith. Not only is the grief healthy, but the process of
grieving is crucial for recovery, for through it we are able to
separate from what has been lost. Jesus, though knowing he

was going to resurrect Lazarus from the dead, nonetheless, wept and grieved with those around him. And for us also, grief is an appropriate response to death. Do not be ashamed of your sorrow, and do not try to hide it from others.

Grieving occurs in stages. By looking at them you may better understand what you are undergoing. Keep in mind however, that just as each person is unique, your experience will also be unique. Also since there is no set time limit to the grieving process, its phases are not necessarily discrete and separate. You may find yourself going over ground you thought you had already covered, because new circumstances may trigger old memories. As a result, each new situation may be a small grieving experience in itself.

You may feel disoriented, with feelings of numbness and denial. Initially, you may find it difficult to believe this has really happened to you. You may wake up in the morning with a momentary sense of the well-being of life as usual, only to be overcome by the realization that your husband is gone. Intermingled with your disbelief, and continuing when your denial passes, will be anger, perhaps even anger toward your husband for "deserting" you. Such anger is not rational, for your husband did not leave you by choice. However, your feeling *is* real and must be faced rather than denied. You may feel anger towards friends who have not lost a spouse, and believe that they could not genuinely empathize with your grief. Often there is anger towards God, blaming him for the death of someone so important to you. You know life will never be the same, and you are angry that this is so. In all these instances, your anger is a normal reaction to death. To deny it, to pretend it isn't there, or to condemn yourself for it will only prolong its passing.

Physical symptoms also often occur. You might experience apathy, fatigue, insomnia, appetite loss, headaches, and loss of concentration. You may feel unable to organize your life. Even things you have done on a daily basis may seem like overwhelming tasks. Just getting the bills paid might seem insurmountable. Such feelings of helplessness may trigger even more anger. Again it is a normal part of the grieving process, and condemning yourself is counter-productive.

Another characteristic of the grieving process is guilt. As you relive memories of your husband, you may blame yourself for things left undone and unsaid, letting regrets and "if onlys" overpower you. This could be exacerbated if he had a long illness, because certainly there were days when you did not feel up to, or even resented, taking care of your husband. This too is natural. Guilt feelings may be very real to you—and surely no one is immune to them—but let some part of your mind remember that they too are part of grieving. Only God loves perfectly. Remembering that will assuage the harshness of your self-judgment.

You might have questions about God. When our life is shattered we cannot help but ask difficult questions about the One who gives and who also takes away. Not only has he taken your husband away, but often he seems silent in the face of your pain.

C.S. Lewis describes his feelings about God after the death of his wife in his book, *A Grief Observed:* "But go to Him when your need is desperate, when all other help is in vain, and what do you find? A door slammed in your face, and a sound of bolting and double bolting on the inside. After that, silence.... Why is He so present as a commander in our time of prosperity and so very absent a help in time of trouble?"

The feeling that God is not present when we most need him can be powerful and guilt-producing. Many have found comfort in Lewis's words, as they have learned that others, even of the stature of Lewis, have similarly wrestled with such frightening feelings and questions.

Bottling up all that you are experiencing is not healthy, nor is it an indication of strength. God has planted us in the nurturing soil of community because we need each other for support and care. He does not intend for you to grieve alone.

If you do not feel that a good friend can be there for you in a loving, non-judgmental way you might seek help from your pastor or professional counselor. Also, most hospitals can refer you to a grief support group.

Time does heal wounds, but it does *not* eradicate them. Though healthy grieving will enable you to return to the present and invest yourself in people and activities, you will always feel the loss. Lewis describes how that loss continues: "To say a patient is getting over it after an operation for appendicitis is one thing; after he's had his leg off it is quite another. After that operation the wounded stump heals or the man dies. If it heals, the fierce, continuous pain will stop. Presently he'll get back his strength and be able to stump about on his wooden leg. He has 'got over it.' But he will probably have recurrent pains in the stump all his life, and perhaps pretty bad ones; and he will always be a one-legged man.... His whole way of life will be changed.... At present I am learning to get about on crutches. Perhaps I shall presently be given a wooden leg. But I shall never be a biped again." So you too will never have again what is lost, but you will be able to recover from that loss.

Widowed life will be different in a radical way, but that difference does not have to make you a cripple or relegate you to a "half-life." Our God brings life out of death. Perhaps for a time his comfort may seem nonexistent and his silence deafening. But even in the darkness and the silence try to remember that "The Lord is near to the brokenhearted, and saves those who are crushed in spirit" (Psalm 34:19). He *is* near to you, whether you sense his presence or not, and he *will* help you in this time of need.

SEVENTEEN

My Life's Been Turned Upside-down

"I'VE BEEN MARRIED FOR SEVENTEEN YEARS," Cheryl began. "About six months ago I learned that my husband had a son before we were married. The shock was overwhelming. I never even knew he had a sexual relationship with anyone besides me! The boy wants to meet Dave and Dave wants very much to meet him, too. We keep having arguments about this. I'm having great difficulty accepting this news, and wish we could go back to the way things were. I don't want to believe this, nor do I want to accept Dave's son into our lives. I can't see an answer."

It is hard for any of us to face the undeniable and unchangeable. When you have lived a particular life for seventeen years and suddenly basic things you assumed to be true are lost, it can be overwhelming. Cheryl had suddenly discovered that things she assumed to be true about her husband, the person she had been closest to, were not so. Her world was shaken, her loss was irreversible. There was no going back. She could never return to what was. She was faced with facts she could not change. To have our lives turned upside-down overnight is staggering. To learn, for example, that your body is not healthy, but full of cancer, that your child is homosexual, that your unmarried daughter is pregnant; to discover that a trusted friend has betrayed you—all of these events send us into emotional shock.

Initially, most of us fight to deny whatever it is that we ultimately are forced to accept. Everything in us cries out to say that it is not true. Surely our life cannot be so different than we thought it was. Maybe we will wake up tomorrow and everything will be back the way that it was. But when we do wake up each day, we find that the change is undeniably there.

In Cheryl's case, facing change was further complicated because her husband was in a very different place emotionally. He had carried this knowledge in secret for many years, and had wrestled with his guilt and sadness. He had struggled with whether to tell his wife. At the same time he had many questions about his son. His response to renewed contact with him was very different from hers. Cheryl wanted to deny the son's existence, whereas Dave was relieved to some degree that his wife knew, and was eager to see the boy he had thought was out of his life forever.

Unfortunately, it was easy for Cheryl to misconstrue her husband's reaction. It seemed to her that he was oblivious to her pain; she felt pushed aside and not considered, in his eagerness to see his son. It took time for her to understand that the shock she experienced was not shared by him. In his own relief that his secret was out, and in his anticipation of the reunion, he couldn't understand why his wife was having such a struggle. What he had not done was to give her time to adjust to this new and shocking development in their lives.

We often expect others to respond the same way we do. When they withdraw—in contrast to our need to talk constantly—or when they try to minimize when we fear the worst, it is easy to assume they do not care or do not understand. However, we all have unique responses to painful change and if we forget this, we will make erroneous assumptions about those whose support is so important to us.

When the reality of an unalterable and unwelcome situation sets in, we usually find ourselves feeling anger and bitterness. Cheryl's first reaction was hurt over her husband's lack of honesty, and then anger at the big change he had brought into her life. She felt the change was unfair and resented her husband for his responsibility in bringing it about. Many questions were raised in her mind about the basic honesty of her relationship with him.

During a time like this, couples often have repetitive arguments, going over the same ground again and again with no resolution. It feels to them as though they will always be stuck in the same place. However, often during arguments that seem to go nowhere, subtle change and softening are in fact taking place inside. The real issue is what can be done during such a difficult time to encourage growth and change. Obviously, how couples respond to a crisis like this will have great impact on the future of their marriage.

Whenever you come up against a painful and unalterable change, recognize that sadness and shock are legitimate reactions. You are confronting a sad truth. It takes time to adapt. It was difficult for Cheryl to discover that her husband kept the knowledge of something as important as a son from her throughout all their years of intimacy. For seventeen years she had assumed certain things in her life to be true. To learn that they were not true made her question some very basic things about her life and marriage.

Much of your anger, like Cheryl's, will be over your powerlessness to change the discovery. You will keep confronting the enormity of the truth and wanting desperately to make it go away. You will want life to be as it was, and find yourself having to face the fact that it will never again be that way. Your sadness and your anger are part of your grieving over that loss of what was, and will never be again. Anyone whose life has been unalterably changed experiences such a reaction. This kind of grief reaction is evoked whenever bad changes occur, such as the illness or disabling of a spouse, a death in the family, or any difference which prevents life from following the pattern to which we are accustomed. We fight the change through denial, and then with anger. We resent its intrusion in our lives.

One of the ways we learn to accept the unalterable, or unresolvable, is by talking about it over and over again. Each time we "tell the story" we adapt to it a little bit more. We see things a bit differently as we hear ourselves tell what has happened to us. We grow into our new circumstances and eventually learn to wear them a bit more gracefully. Time must pass in order for us to adjust. The support of others who are willing to listen as we work our way through this stage is very important. This support can come from a spouse, but often it needs to be from someone else who is not so affected by the change. If you are single, or if your spouse reacts negatively to your retelling of "the story," make sure you find a friend and/or professional who can help support you and listen to you.

If you must face reconciling yourself to the unalterable and unwelcome, keep in mind two important things. One is given to us by the writer of Hebrews. We are told to "See to it that no one comes short of the grace of God; that no root of bitterness springing up causes trouble, and by it many be defiled" (Hebrews 12:15). The imagery in this verse is powerful. Bitterness is pictured for us as a root, something that penetrates deeply into our being. From the root springs only trouble, which touches many in a hurtful way. Bitterness is not something we can carry in our hearts without detriment to ourselves and others as well.

When we face the unalterable in life, bitterness is a natural human reaction. We seem to have the idea that life should treat us fairly and we demand that it yields what we want. Life in this world is not only often unfair, it is unpredictable. We often get what we do not want. As Christians, we are called to respond without bitterness. This may be no easy matter, but a long, hard battle instead. To face change in your life with courage and honesty, you will have to keep bringing your heart before God, allowing him to show you if the root of bitterness is still within.

The other important point on which to focus is found in Malachi 3:6: "For I, the Lord, do not change"; and again, in James 1:17: "... the Father of lights, with whom there is no variation or shifting shadow." But unlike the one constant, which is God, everything in life does change: our circumstances, other people, and we ourselves. It is the nature of life in this world that nothing is permanent. But knowledge of the changing nature of life does not make it less difficult for most of us to accept. We may prefer routine and predictability because it gives us a sense of control. But we know that the only thing in life that is unalterable is God himself.

When everything in life seems turned upside-down, continually remind yourself of the constancy and permanence of God. He knows about the change you are facing. He knew that you would be forced to face the unalterable and he knew the pain it would cause you. Throughout all of these changes, and through any change yet to come, he remains unchanging. Hold to this truth while you face the fact that life will be forever different. Perhaps you yourself will be different as well, and for the better. This experience, terrible as it is for you now, can help you learn to accept the many changes we all must confront in life.

EIGHTEEN

My Husband and I Don't Agree on How to Rear Our Children

WOMEN FREQUENTLY COME TO ME with frustrations over parenting. A very common story goes something like this:

"We have three children and my husband and I are having a hard time working together as a team. I think he's too harsh with the children and he thinks I'm too easy. We're forever disagreeing about how to discipline the kids. We know this is wrong, but how do we deal with it?"

There are no two ways about it—parenting is difficult. Two people with different personalities, backgrounds, and expectations are somehow supposed to work together smoothly and present some kind of unified front. Is this a reasonable expectation? And if it is, how is it possible?

It is not within the scope of this chapter to consider all of the how-to's of parenting. Rather, let's look at a few questions which all too few parents consider: What is the purpose of your parenting? Why are you doing what you're doing? What is it you hope to accomplish?

Most of us, if we are honest, will admit to mixed motives in having and raising children. Some of us had children simply because it was that time in life. Or perhaps we wanted someone to love and nurture, or to depend on and love us. Maybe some of us wanted to have a piece of ourselves to leave behind after we're gone.

When our motives are mixed, so is our purpose. We get angry and frustrated when our children do not act the way we want, or when we think they make us look bad in front of others. We get upset, even afraid, when it seems that they do not love us, or when we feel like we do not love them. Many of these difficulties are the result of having an unclear purpose.

What should our purpose be? It is, I think, clearly stated for us in Genesis 18:19. God has just visited with Abraham and Sarah to affirm for them his promise of a son. As God and Abraham are walking toward Sodom, the Lord says that he will not hide from Abraham what he is about to do. God says he has "chosen him, in order that he might command his children and his household after him to keep the way of the Lord by doing righteousness and justice."

That is the purpose of parenting—to teach our children to keep the way of the Lord by doing righteousness and justice. Everything that you and your husband do, should be for the purpose of teaching your children to keep the way of the Lord.

How are we to do this? The answer has two components—the first, a general one; the second, more specific. Let's first look at the broader answer, which is again found in Scripture. We are told in Deuteronomy 6 that Moses gave us a commandment, which God himself commanded him to teach. The purpose of it is that we, along with our children, might fear the Lord and obey him.

So what Moses is about to tell us is God's own "how-to" regarding the carrying out of his purpose for parenting. The first aspect of that directive is to parents that they must "love the Lord your God with all your heart and with all your soul and with all your might." If you want to carry out God's purpose in your relationship to your children, then love God with everything you have. The first part has nothing to do with your children at all; nurture, strengthen, and guard *your* relationship with God above all else. That is the first and most important thing you can do to carry out God's purpose in the lives of your children.

As you do that you will recognize that they are *his* children, not yours. They are a gift to you, given in order that you might carry out God's purpose in their lives. When you focus first on your relationship to God, he will purify your motives regarding your children. You will begin to find freedom from the entanglement of mixed motives.

As that happens you will naturally begin to carry out the more specific aspect of God's command, which is an outgrowth of loving God with all your heart. As you concentrate on loving him, you will carry his words in your heart and will "teach them diligently to your children and shall talk of them when you sit in your house and when you walk by the way and when you lie down and when you rise up." Your parenting will flow out of your relationship to God himself, and that relationship will infiltrate everything that you do.

Now how does all this relate to the difficulties mentioned in the beginning of this chapter? How can two people, so different in personality and parenting ideas, work together so *God's* purpose is accomplished? First, if you and your husband both really grasp the fact that God's purpose for parenting is what is important, then you immediately will see that you are not at odds with each other. You both are subject to God's perspective on your children and how to raise them. It ceases to be "my way" versus "your way," and becomes a quest for "our way" as subject to God. No longer is the question, "Shall we do it my softer way, or your harder way?" Instead it becomes, "How can both our ways be used together to accomplish God's purpose?"

The focus has ceased to be one of determining who is

right, especially since it is usually safe to assume that neither parent is exactly right nor wrong. Usually both parents have a piece of the response that is necessary. But how can you put them together so you can better approximate how God relates to us? Unless you consider how to combine your responses, you will be at odds with one another. Framing it this way will cause you to come together before God.

As you come together before God with your parenting, you will find that you share not only a common purpose, but also a common how-to. Paul expresses it clearly in Ephesians 4:15: ". . . speaking the truth in love." The literal translation is "truthing it in love." There is a beautiful balance in that verse. Truth is often harsh and blunt; reality can be ugly. We are, however, called to "truth it." Love without truth can be weak, and not honest. We are however, called to love. These are to be done in tandem. We are to live truly, walk truly, communicate truly—in love. Perhaps your husband is off balance in his hardness, or you are off balance in your softness. God's way includes truth and love, straightforwardness and gentleness, justice and mercy.

A specific way you can "truth it" before your children is to let them see some of your struggles in this area. So often parents have the mistaken idea that presenting a unified front means never disagreeing about anything. That is not real life. It is not truth. The truth is that people disagree. The question is, not whether Christians *may* disagree, but *how* they should disagree.

Let your children hear that you sometimes think differently. Let them hear that you take your individual opinions before God and subject them to him. Let them see that your unity is not found in simply reflecting the opinion of the other or in just giving up your own, but rather your unity is found in a shared purpose.

Show them that you have the shared purpose of teaching them the way of the Lord, as well as that of learning to love him more yourselves. Instruct by the example of your life together that this matters above all else. It is not most important that Mom get her way regarding discipline, or that Dad get his way. It is most crucial that Mom and Dad together continually subject their responses to God, considering the other and being willing to be taught through the other. There is so little of this unity in the church today! What a marvelous opportunity to model it for your children!

Unity, when there is complete agreement, is not a challenge. Unity in spite of difference is what God has called us to. Paul in Ephesians 4 shows that the result of "truthing it in love" is the "growth of the body for the building up of itself in love."

As you work to parent together in this fashion, you will see growth in your family. Teach your children to keep the way of the Lord by loving the Lord your God with all *your* heart, and by speaking the truth in love every day of your life.

Part Three

A Woman and Her Family

NINETEEN

But I Don't Want Another Baby!

K AREN IS SPENDING ALL HER WAKING HOURS attending to the needs of her young family. She has three children, all under the age of five. Barely coping, she now finds herself pregnant with an unplanned child. The demands on her are relentless, the positive feedback rare, and the opportunities for pursuing her own interests limited. It is a sacrificial life, as she is constantly called on to meet the needs of others without regard for her own. She finds nothing glamorous about pushing one tired foot after another up the stairs to discipline a naughty child, nor anything enlightening about getting up at three o'clock in the morning because something hurts. And there are many days that feel like a comedy of errors, when she goes from wiping up one spilled mess after another to handling emergencies—like the baby falling and needing stitches or the washing machine breaking down in the rinse cycle.

Motherhood is trying enough when each and every baby is planned and desired. But add another child, unplanned and unwanted, and you have the ingredients for a big problem. Karen's feelings were understandably angry and ambivalent, because this pregnancy had begun when she was already exhausted and overwhelmed.

Glad as she was to see her husband at night, his coming and going required adapting by both her and the children. She wanted him to come home to an atmosphere of calm, greeted by a serene wife, happy kids, and a welcoming dinner. Now that was hard to pull off; she was dealing with all the physical changes that pregnancy brings, along with nurturing inside her a new and totally dependent life. No wonder Karen wanted to run away and never look back!

Before Karen and I looked at some practical suggestions that might help, I asked her to consider the whole area of attitude. At the moment she had some feelings of resentment, anger, and fear. It was important to understand the causes of those unwanted feelings. We discovered two things (common, by the way) contributed to her negative attitude. She felt inadequate. She was already overwhelmed by daily demands. She certainly had good reason to feel inadequate without the prospect of a new baby in the future. She felt inadequate physically, for her body had hardly had time to recover from previous pregnancies before it entered into this new one. Added to her general tiredness was the fact that her small children often interrupted her sleep. In addition to feeling emotionally and physically unable to cope with all the demands in her life, she felt spiritually inadequate as well.

This pregnancy was an intrusion in Karen's life. She did not desire it, nor did she plan it and she was afraid she couldn't handle it. Not only was it not according to her plans, it seemed in direct opposition to them. When we feel out of control both fear and anger are common reactions, and Karen was angry and afraid.

We feel trapped when things are not the way we want them to be. We live under the illusion that we can control our own lives until we wake up one morning and face such an intrusion as an unwanted pregnancy. We respond with anger and questions. How could this be? God has given me more than I can bear. How can I manage? Why did it happen to me, especially now, when I was already trying so hard?

If you are another Karen, how can changing your attitude alleviate your stress? For one thing, I think you need to recognize that your feelings of inadequacy and intrusion are justified. No woman feels completely adequate for the task of mothering. Whether one child or ten, it's a demanding responsibility. And a new baby *will* be an intrusion into your life. Even the most wanted baby is an intrusion, upsetting schedules, knowing only his or her own needs. Some babies are welcomed intrusions, but all are intrusions, for they certainly do not make their demands based on our convenience!

Recognizing that you have these feelings of anger, fear, and inadequacy can help relieve some of your tension. The real problem, you see, is not the baby, although on a practical level, it is. Your real problem arises from your fear about and bitterness toward those circumstances which have caused you to feel angry and inadequate. The baby is the catalyst being used to reveal something about you to yourself. Your primary struggle is not really with your pregnancy, but rather with the fact that God has said that under no set of circumstances are we to let fear or bitterness control us. Your pregnancy is indeed overwhelming, but God says even here you are not to let the fear or bitterness control you. The reason he gives is that these things not only hurt us, but also reach out and hurt others. In your case, it will grow and touch the lives of all of your children, and your husband as well.

Be honest with God about your sense of inadequacy. He knows you are inadequate, and does not demand that you be otherwise. Paul says "that we are not adequate in ourselves to consider anything as *coming* from ourselves, but our adequacy is from God" (2 Corinthians 3:5). He also tells us that God's grace is sufficient, because his power is made perfect against the backdrop of our weakness. If you bring your inadequacy to God, you will have offered him the ideal background against which he can display his power.

Intrusion—just what does that mean? It means something has occurred in your life which is not to your liking and is a major inconvenience. It is interesting that when good things happen we call them blessings, and when hard things happen we call them intrusions or injustices.

God intrudes into our lives all the time. We only complain when we don't agree with how he chooses to do so! One of the most difficult battles for us as Christians is in the area of trust. God is always bringing us through circumstances that call for a deeper level of trust than we have yet experienced. The only way trust seems to deepen is through hard times, walking where we cannot see, and feeling insufficient to handle whatever we're facing. God has asked you to respond with trust to an intrusion that causes you to feel inadequate. It is a hard lesson, but as you struggle with it, you will become more like Christ. And that, I believe, is God's intention.

Practically speaking, you need to take some measures to make your circumstances as manageable as possible. First, remember that though a pregnancy can seem interminable, it is but a brief season in your life. There will be other times and other seasons, each bringing their respective struggles and joys. In light of this, once the baby comes, you and your husband need to seriously discuss what you want to do about birth control. Clearly, whatever you were doing is not foolproof! If you truly believe that you cannot handle any more children, then you might even want to consider something like a tubal ligation when you deliver this baby, something that would need to be discussed very carefully.

Second, you really need some practical help from others. I would not hesitate to let your needs be known at church. The body of Christ is there to encourage and support, and both you and your husband will need that ministry. You are going to need help with meals and the children not only when the new baby arrives, but also in the future. Accept the help graciously. You can return the favor in the future to another young mother.

Finally, you and your husband will need to maintain good communication or else you will have fertile ground for problems in your marriage. This new baby will be hard on both of you, but in very different ways. It is very easy to be so caught up in your own hardship that you lose sight of your spouse's because it is not the same as yours. He will walk in the door from a business trip and you will want instant relief from the children. He, on the other hand, will want to simply rest and have some quiet time. You will need to find a compromise in order to meet both your needs, to the extent that it is possible. That will require careful discussion and planning, underscored by a respect for what is really important to each of you, and what realistically can be done.

I would like to close with the thought that life is full of surprises, and what often seems disastrous turns out instead to be a marvelous blessing. The following is a letter written by a ninety-one-year-old mother to her daughter on her sixty-fifth birthday. The daughter to whom this was written was with her twin, the fourth and fifth babies born to her young mother, who soon found herself burying one and then raising the four remaining children as a single parent during the Depression.

"Happy Birthday to My Unwanted Baby,
    If that is not a funny birthday greeting, you will have to admit that it is original.
    It was brought to my mind because of all the talk, by the pro-abortionists, about these poor unwanted babies who will be unwanted and unloved all the rest of their lives.... This mother began to love you when she first felt movement, if not before.
    I got to thinking about what a cute baby you were. Did I ever tell you what I called you when you were a year or so old? "Little Curly-locks-dipped-in-gold," because your

TWENTY

I Love My Children—
It's Me I Don't Like

T AKING CARE OF SMALL CHILDREN is an interesting, reward-
ing and exhausting way to spend a portion of one's life.
Most women spend a significant part of their adulthood
doing just that. They give birth to utterly helpless human
beings, and then proceed to spend years nurturing, disci-
plining, and loving them. But this relationship of intense caring, while bringing with it many rewards and much
fulfillment, can exact heavy payment in terms of a woman's
self-image.

The immediate effect of giving birth to an infant is that it
decreases the size of the mother's world. This is particularly
true if the mother, like most women, has worked prior to
giving birth. But it is also true even for those who have not
worked. Exhaustion limits a young mother's capacity to be
involved in many things, and the child certainly limits her
mobility. Obviously, the more children one has, the more this
is true.

Not only is her world smaller, but many previous sources
of satisfaction are no longer available for her. The pleasure
once derived from a job is gone, as well as the sense of com-
petence, intellectual stimulation, and the positive feedback
from advancement in a career. Too, the new mother has less
time and energy for pursuits and relationships that had pre-

viously had a good effect on her self-image. In short, the young woman has left behind a good tennis game or a stimulating conversation, in order to devote her time to laundry and dirty diapers. Somehow the exchange is not an equal one!

Her life today consists of routine that is daily, basic, and often mundane. All of our lives necessitate a great deal of routine tasks, but dependent babies demand attention in an urgent and unrelenting fashion. No longer is there the flexibility to go out, entertain, or cook something out of the ordinary. Nursing every three hours, cleaning up spilled juice or spewed out spinach becomes a total way of life with little or no relief.

One of the ways we derive satisfaction from any work is through positive feedback and approval of others. As they respond with appreciation we know we have done our job well. Clearly, this is not something that occurs with small children. They make most of their demands known, you meet them, and then they have other needs which must be met, and still others, over and over again. No gratitude is forthcoming. There are rewards from childrearing in terms of feedback, but they are also slow in coming. And the more we have the need for a positive response from those we are serving, the harder it becomes to find satisfaction. How can you know you are doing a good job, when the "product" is not anywhere near completion?

All of these factors contribute to frustration, depression, and insecurity on the part of a young mother. Depression is more common among stay-at-home young mothers than any other group in our country.

In view of this, what can you do to avoid having these factors eat away at your self-esteem? Before giving some practical suggestions, I would like to suggest two attitudes which may alter the way you view mothering and the expectations you have of your relationships with your children.

Many mothers have been taught that any effort to care for themselves is selfish and wrong. The more you have "given up" your own life, and the more that your life is literally dictated by the needs of the children, the better mother you are considered to be. Many women have bought into this and literally do nothing except those things which relate to their children. Obviously, their personal lives and marriages suffer serious damage as they have become less than the well-rounded persons their husbands married. Some feel that to pursue an individual interest, or to put off the children for the sake of the husband, is selfish, and selfishness is a mother's greatest sin.

What an intimidating and destructive view! It reduces women to their biological nature. Both men and women are called by God to be fruitful. Both men and women are called to rule the earth. Scripture, while placing great emphasis on parenting, never reduces men or women to that role only. Jesus made that abundantly clear in his affirmation of Mary's choice to sit at his feet and learn.

This view is harmful to children as well, for it means they are nurtured by driven, guilt-ridden women who have no life other than that of their children who now bear full responsibility for their mother's "success."

God has called all of us to deepen our relationship with him and with each other continually. Mothers have been gifted by God to build up the body of his church. Certainly one of the ways women can do that is through effective mothering, but that is not the only way. Children need to see mothers who are balanced in the way they live out their lives. They need mothers whom they can watch actively seeking to deepen their relationship with Christ, mothers who encourage others, and mothers who responsibly handle the gifts God has given them for the nurturing of his body.

An effective mother is one who continually works at growing in discipline, patience, and balance. Neglect of herself will not result in such a mother. In making women multifaceted, God has given them their greatest tool for mothering. He wants to use who we are to teach our children about himself and about life in this world. Mothers who do not nurture themselves are not helping their children learn about God and life.

We may go into parenting expecting intimacy with children to be a smaller version of intimacy with adults. The mother-child relationship is a rich one with many rewards, but these rewards are very different from those found in the professional world. When this is not understood, the transition to motherhood becomes both difficult and disappointing to many women.

Articulate feedback does not come from small children; they do not praise good mothering. Needless to say, they do not promote you either. Rather, their rewards come in the form of sticky hands reaching up for a hug, an indecipherable picture given with pride, or a bedtime prayer. Their rewards are real and can touch us deeply. If we are looking for other rewards, these tokens from our children can easily get lost in the routine of the day. When this happens, the sticky hands are greeted with, "Oh, look what you've done to my clothes!" The indecipherable picture gets a mindless, "Mm, that's nice." The bedtime prayer is seen as another chore of the day. Then the rewards are lost on us, we have not let ourselves be touched, and we feel unappreciated and unacknowledged.

How can you avoid these pitfalls, enjoy motherhood, and survive with your self-esteem intact? One way is to make sure your life is not reduced to motherhood. Prize your children, yes, but protect your intimacy with your husband. Do things that remind you that you are *first* husband and wife, before you are father and mother. Pursue a hobby or interest that is separate from your children. Remember that you and your children are distinct persons, and make sure that you act on that, developing friendships with other young mothers, as well as with women in different circumstances.

Another important thing to do is to nurture your own personal and spiritual growth. We cannot teach our children about God unless we know him ourselves in a living, ever-growing way. Likewise, we cannot discipline our children effectively unless we discipline ourselves. So many young mothers cease to be disciplined in their own eating and exercise habits. How can we then model discipline for our children?

Do not put yourself aside as if you do not matter, as if you are something that you will take out and look at again when your children are grown. God has called us to be like Ruth, of whom Boaz said, "And now, my daughter, do not fear. I will do for you whatever you ask, for all my people in the city know that you are a woman of excellence" (Ruth 3:11). Pursue excellence as a mother, but pursue it also as a person, a wife, and a woman gifted by God.

I usually encourage young mothers to take up some interest that provides concrete, immediate, and positive feedback. This can be a sport, gardening, handwork, or anything you can step back from relatively quickly and see a job well done.

If you do these things, the season of your life as a mother, though very different from that as a career woman, will be rich with rewards. Motherhood can indeed contribute, and not detract from your self-esteem. You will have many happy memories when you move on to a new season.

TWENTY-ONE

Should I Work Outside the Home?

THE TOPIC OF WORKING MOTHERS is an important one these days, because women have more choices and higher expectations for themselves. Rather than engage in a discussion of whether or not mothers "should" work (outside the home), I'd like to focus on how women can handle their roles—whatever they may be—in a responsible way.

All mothers work. Some work in one or two arenas, such as, home and church. Others work in several—home, church, profession, or community. My focus will not be on what arenas of "work" are appropriate for mothers, but rather, how should mothers think about their work? To answer, let's first look at what a sound perspective on work is.

Work is both good and necessary. As women, we are made in the image of God, who is himself a worker. Both Adam and Eve were created by God, placed in Eden and given the responsibility of work. God's work was good, and their work was good. Then the man and woman were banished from the garden, still under the directive to work. Work now was hard, often bringing pain and bearing blemished fruit. After the Fall, work became like the man and woman—flawed.

However, even in the midst of the pain and struggle due to sin, God promised redemption. That redemption, which came in the person of Jesus Christ, was to bring life out of death, fruitfulness instead of barrenness. God's redemptive action touches all aspects of our lives, work included. Therefore, our purpose in every arena is to be fruitful to the glory of God. Paul tells us this in several places, such as 1 Corinthians 10:31: "Whether, then, you eat or drink or whatever you do, do all to the glory of God."

If this is true, it should change the questions we ask about work. For example, "Should women (or mothers) work?" becomes "What work would God have me to do?" And, "How am I to do that work to the glory of God?"

All of us have not been given the same work, anymore than we have all been given the same gifts. Each of us is uniquely gifted, and uniquely called. Even given the same work, no two of us would do it the same way. Our God is a God of diversity, whether that be in the patterns of frost on a window, or the patterns of giftedness in his people. What are the implications of this?

If the sum of my life is that I am to become more and more like Christ, and hence glorify God, then my first "work" is my relationship to Christ. This is illustrated in the gospel story of Mary and Martha. Martha's work was not wrong. Someone had to cook a meal for all those hungry people. It was a service to do so and we are called to serve others. Her error was not in her work, but in her misdirected focus. To Martha, her work was central, an end in itself. Christ said her relationship to him was to be central. She was distracted and bothered because her focus was wrong.

How often those words describe women today! We are distracted, worried, harried, bothered by many things. Jesus says he is to be central. He did not tell Martha not to cook or serve. But service, even "spiritual" service that is central, distracts us from our purpose. Mary chose a different route, and Jesus said she chose "the good part."

Parenthetically, what Mary chose (sitting at a teacher's feet) was only acceptable for men in that culture. Clearly, Jesus did not think cultural or religious norms are to determine what is good or right for women (or men for that matter). Martha chose what was culturally acceptable, and Mary did not. Jesus cut right through that and said that such norms were not the point at all.

Jesus operated from a completely different set of values. The first priority is to be our relationship to God. Jesus demonstrated faithfulness to his own teaching for he often left needy people to be alone with God in prayer. Unlike many of us, he was not *ruled* by the needs of others, even as he was not indifferent to them. Martha, ruled by the needs of those around her, became distracted and bothered. To choose that way is not to choose the good part.

It is possible to be a godly working mother then, if you continually choose that which is good. Maintain a growing relationship with Christ no matter what the cost. To do so will mean doing less in the hectic world. Knowing exactly where that "less" will be, will require great wisdom. It may mean less in your career, less in your church involvement, less socially, or in your community. You may at first feel guilty about things you say "no" to, but it is more important that you guard your time to sit at Jesus' feet. And you'll be surprised to discover that your other work will still get done!

Does every "good" choice glorify God? For example, suppose you have been asked to teach a Sunday school class. "Yes, I will" sounds right, but is it? Wouldn't it be for God's glory, since the class is in and for his church?

Where the work takes place does not determine whether or not it is to the glory of God. There are many men and women today whose families suffer because of their over-involvement in the church. Just because activity takes place in the church does not insure that it will bring glory to God. Of course, God has called us to work in the body of believers; I do not deny that. Often, however, our decisions to do so are dictated by the needs of other people. We are certainly to meet others' needs, often in a sacrificial way. But needs are endless, and if they alone motivate us we will never say no. Remember, Martha was serving Jesus, but her work was not "spiritual" in the true sense of the word.

On a practical level, pray before saying "yes" or "no," even to "good" causes. Whether your career work, your church work, or your children's activities (for that is their work), you and your family should discuss its impact on the individual, his or her relationship to God, and on the family as a whole. What changes will be required of other family members? Will someone have to take time to drive? Will someone have to pick up extra chores at home? Will there be less family time? Can all those things be done in a way that glorifies God?

We are not given an unlimited amount of time or energy. Time is allotted to us in finite amounts and we need to exercise wisdom in how we spend it. The amount we have of both time and energy varies at different periods of our lives. A young mother has less of both to spare than the woman whose children have grown and moved on. If we allow the busyness that leads to distraction and worry, we will lose the gentle things in life. If you lose the ability to listen with leisure to your child's story or your husband's trials at work, then you have lost gentle things.

The temptation will always be there to judge the success of your life by the success of your career or by the success of your involvement at church or in the community. Paul says in 1 Corinthians 3:13, that the day will come when "each man's work will become evident; for the day will disclose it, because it is to be revealed with fire; and the fire itself will test the quality of each man's work."

Yours will withstand that test as long as you know that your motivation is to be like Christ and glorify God. Let that aim govern how you spend every minute, so that with Christ you can say, "I glorified Thee on the earth, having accomplished the work which Thou hast given Me to do" (John 17:4).

During parenthood, the bulk of your work will be caring for your family. Do not neglect your family by doing too much outside of it. Later, the balance will shift and you will be freed to serve a larger world. At whatever season, choose the good part. Let nothing hinder your relationship with the Giver of work. It is only at his feet that you will find the wisdom needed to balance the many tasks which he has called you to.

TWENTY-TWO

Does Being an "At-Home Mom" Make Me Second Class?

I T IS INTERESTING HOW THE TERM "working mother" has come to mean the mother who also works outside the home. Even the preceding chapter uses that term, as if to imply that the mother who is at home full time, keeping house and raising children, is not working. Nothing could be further from the truth. (Actually the previous chapter dealt with the nature of a woman's work, not its locale.)

Are you concerned that you, as a "stay-at-home" mom, are somehow second-class compared to those who work outside? Even though you are happy with your choice, and readily accept the budget limitations, you may fight the smallness of your world and wonder if what you do in it is really significant.

Many mothers—used to adult conversation and intellectual stimulation in the academic or business world—ask the same thing. Unused to being home with a little one, they are lonely in neighborhoods emptied by "working women." Many of their negative feelings about staying home stem from the current controversy over "working mothers" versus those who stay at home. Women on each side may justify their position by claiming it is the only godly one for

Christian mothers. This has caused great division in the church, and any attitude which is divisive is not of the Spirit. The action of the Holy Spirit in our lives produces unity and mutual encouragement. All mothers have a tremendous task in today's world. How sad that women who claim the name of Jesus quarrel with each other!

Scripture does not lay out a timeless blueprint for all women. God has said that those of us who are mothers are to be "home-lovers" (Titus 2:5, Phillips), or as the Amplified version states it, "makers of a home." We will not all do this in the same way. Some women add to the "homeyness" of their homes through the gifts they have in their hands. Some do it in the way they bring beautiful music into the lives of their families. All of us are to do it by the ways we love our husbands and children. That we love them to the glory of God is to be clearly evident. To do so does not necessarily mean staying at home all the time, anymore than working outside the home makes one a better woman. Anything that hinders our loving of our husband and children should be eliminated. For you that may mean different things than for your neighbor, and neither of you is to criticize the other.

When there is an atmosphere of criticism all of us feel somewhat uncertain, even defensive, about our choices. Women who are at home feel judged as inferior by those who are not, while women in the work force feel judged as uncaring mothers by those at home. To allay our fears, we compete and say things like, "I'm doing this better," or, "My life style allows me to...," or "I have so much more because I've chosen..."

Paul says that those who "measure themselves by their own standards or by comparisons within their own circle don't make accurate estimations, you may be sure." He adds: "No, we shall not make any wild claims, but simply judge ourselves by that line of duty which God has marked out for us, and that line includes our work on your behalf" (2 Corinthians 10:12-13, Phillips).

So, do not concern yourself with the judgments of others. You have considered the options and decided being an "at-home mom" is best for your family. Many studies have shown the great psychological value of a mother staying home with very young children. Infants and small children are dependent and vulnerable, thus security and love are crucial elements in their development.

You and your husband have made a choice about your family before God. It is his judgment and his praise that should concern you, not those of others. He has called you to be a "home-lover." Honor him in the way you carry out that calling. Do not compare yourself to others and the way they have responded to the same call.

If the criticism of others becomes burdensome, lovingly confront them. You might say something like this: "I appreciate the fact that God has worked differently in your life and mine. He has however, called both of us to care for our families to his glory, as well as to be a support to each other in that task. When you are so critical of how I have chosen to respond to that call, I find myself torn down rather than built up. Couldn't we work together to find a way to encourage one another, even though our paths are so different?"

Such a response is difficult because in the face of criticism we tend to respond with defensiveness and want to retaliate. But you can avoid this type of reaction if you keep in mind that you are doing the work God has called you to do. Furthermore, you can honor him by your response to those who would be your judge.

Another thing which I would encourage you to keep in mind is that the validity of your work is not determined by *what* you are doing, but rather by the manner in which it is carried out. Your struggles with the routine of your days might cause you to wonder if you are operating below capacity. Is capacity determined by the amount of things one is doing? That is clearly not the case, for there are those who are doing so many things that the sheer amount itself is what keeps them from operating at full capacity!

Capacity is determined by the way you give yourself to any task. Every time you give your best to any task or person as unto the Lord, then you are operating at full capacity. This is as true when you are changing a diaper as it is when you are teaching a class. It is as true when you are caring for a toddler's scraped knee as it is when you are conducting a committee meeting.

All work done in the body is our spiritual service of worship. No one's work is more valuable than another's. I would encourage you to present the routine of your days, even the "smallness" of your world to God as a sacrifice acceptable to him. It is acceptable, not because it is grand or showy, but because it is done in Jesus' name, and to the glory of God.

TWENTY-THREE

I Am a Single Mother

S INGLE PARENTING IS OVERWHELMING. Often it is coupled with the equally difficult problem of grieving for a spouse lost through death or divorce. Children must also cope with loss, for they now have only one parent on hand. The single mother now must function alone, without the presence and support of a man. Her loss is great, her task overwhelming.

Single mothers often have the mistaken idea that they must be both mother and father to their children. Try not to place such a burden on yourself. You cannot function as father. You are not a man, nor are you a father. You are a woman and a mother, and that is all you can be. It is also all that God expects you to be. So often in these circumstances others glibly (and thoughtlessly) say, "Now you must be both father and mother." But the fact of the matter is that for now your children have no father in their home, whether that is because you have lost your husband through death or divorce, or because you began parenting as a single person. That is a harsh truth, but it *is* the truth. To expect that you can somehow make it untrue by serving as both parents is impossibly burdensome for you and unrealistic for your children.

This is not to say that you will not need and want to do some of the things that a father might do. There will certainly be chores and activities which fall on you that may have once been his. Since some of these things will seem awkward to you, and add to your responsibilities as well, it is important that you carefully scrutinize and evaluate new demands. Also ask yourself, "what can I eliminate that's no longer necessary?" You need more time and energy to care for your family now than you did before, and you have only a limited amount of both. Obviously, your task is greater than it was. This is especially so if you have also become the breadwinner for your family. In any case, you are responsible for seeing that bills are paid.

Why not sit down with your kids and let them help figure out what things are most important to all of you? If they really want you to attend sports events, and that is something your husband typically did, then clearly that amount of time must be taken from somewhere else. If your children have input regardingfamily priorities, they will be more likely to accept what has happened.

You must fight the idea that somehow you must "make up" for your children's emotional loss. If you try to do this, again you will burden yourself unnecessarily. Nothing you do can make their lives seem as if there is no loss. One of the hardest aspects of parenting is watching our children be hurt by the harsh realities of life. We instinctively want to shield them. However, to protect them by pretense is not helpful. Letting go, even in small matters, is often hard. And a child's loss of a parent is hardly small! Even so, your children will have to face it in their own way, and work through their own loss, just as you must. You can help them in this difficult process, but you cannot do it for them, much as you would like to. Even if you could, it would not be good for them.

Some single parents run themselves ragged with their children's activities, or spend money lavishly, in attempts to make life continue as if the loss had never occurred, or to help their children not feel "different" from two-parent households. But their home *is* different. Their lives are altered, as is yours. Try not to allow yourself to be hounded by the belief that you must at all costs make up to them for what has been taken away. You cannot.

What are some positive things to strive toward with your children? The first is to keep before you a realistic picture of the kind of home you want your children to experience. I am sure that you want to nurture an atmosphere of warmth, caring, and serving—attributes God calls for in all our relationships. Every decision you make regarding time and activities needs to be governed by this goal. Continually model for your children the attitude Paul stresses in Philippians 2:4: "Do look out for your own personal interests, but also each for the interests of others." With this in mind, you can develop as a family into a harmonious unit that nurtures the growth of all its members.

Second, achieve a balance between your responsibility to your children and your responsibility to yourself. If you allow yourself to try to make up for your children's loss, or to make their adjustment for them, you will have to ignore your responsibility to yourself. This will not only hurt you, but your children as well. They need to see in you a model for a healthy adult, with interests and friendships that are separate from theirs. This will help to keep them from feeling responsible for your happiness, a burden many children of single parents feel. Another reason you need these outside interests in your life is to replenish your reservoirs of love and joy. If you do nothing but work and take care of them, there will be nothing in your life which nurtures or feeds you. You will find yourself feeling empty and depleted, with nothing to give your children but impatience and annoyance. This aspect of emotional health is important for all parents, but particularly for single parents, because of the greater physical and emotional demands on them.

The third positive thing to work on is finding a support network for both you and your children. One would hope that you could find such a network in your local church, but if not, there are other avenues to pursue. Your children need to be involved with other adults who can be there for them and listen to them. It is especially crucial that they have concerned men in their lives. Boys need men to serve as models for them, and girls need men to help them learn how to develop healthy male relationships in the future. This will also be a help to you, because you must be able to share the burden of single parenting. There will be many times in your children's growing up when they will not want to listen to you. To be able to fall back at such times on trusted adults will mean the world to you.

You also need a network of friends to support, encourage, and have fun with you. You need places where you can go and just be an adult without the responsibility of your family. Also, you will sometimes require help around the house. Do not hesitate to make such needs known to your church, for helping mothers without mates is a clear scriptural call to the church.

Though your loss is great, and your task difficult, be aware of the importance of not placing unrealistic expectations on yourself. Continually remind yourself to be content with just being the best person you can be, the best *mother* you can be—no more, no less. And finally, enjoy your children.

TWENTY-FOUR

I Don't Understand My Adopted Child

A DOPTION PROVIDED MARTI A WONDERFUL OPPORTUNITY to serve two very real human needs—that of hers to love and nurture a child, and the need of a helpless and vulnerable baby to be raised in her loving and nurturing home. But no one warned Marti that raising an adopted child has its own particular problems, especially since she also had natural children.

Adolescence, when all children search out their own identities, turned out to be the most troubling period for Marti's adopted daughter. The normal parent-child conflict escalated as the girl became convinced that Marti and her husband could not truly love her, and that somewhere out there she had natural parents who could love her more fully and understand her needs. Marti couldn't help being threatened by this response to her discipline, and feared that her daughter's quest for her "real" mother would cause her to lose her.

The foremost problem faced by the mother of an adopted child is the same one faced by most parents of adolescents: Mutual lack of understanding. This already difficult period is exacerbated by the child's yearning for her natural mother, and by the adoptive mother's fear of losing her. Let's deal with this crisis by sorting out the issues involved, and address each separately to see how each impacts on the other.

Every child, adopted or not, is different, and therefore each goes through developmental stages in a unique way. It is important not to assume that differences in the way natural and adopted children maneuver through adolescence are the result of their different birth status. These discrepancies are more likely the result of their individual personalities. Some children seem to sail through adolescence while their parents sing their praises, usually convinced that it is a result of their superb parenting. Other adolescents have a bumpy time of it, careening their way through five to ten years, and adding at least that many to their parents' age. Unfortunately, even intelligent and sensitive parents assume that these "growing pains" are due to their having made terrible mistakes. They are sure that if they had only done more things right (and often they have no idea what), then this turmoil could have been avoided. If there is a natural child in the household, and particularly if that child is not presenting problems, it is tempting to assume that the root of the problem is in the birth status.

But this is not necessarily the case. Each child finds his way to independence in his own unique fashion. Each will need his or her parents to work hard at understanding his or her particular ways of doing so. One child may be able to smoothly detach from dependence and almost seem to wake up an adult on his own. The other may mature in a turbulent fashion. But both are working toward independence, and although each goes about it differently, both are moving in the right direction.

Obviously, each will elicit different responses from you as any two children would. It is crucial not to compare or judge one way as the right way, because it is less troublesome, and the other the wrong because it is so difficult for you. Your response to either will need to be wisdom and firmness. Certainly you will have to discipline behavior that is clearly wrong. That is not, however, the same as punishing a child for his own personal style, even when that style makes you feel less adequate as a parent. It is critical that you see the difference between responding differently, and responding judgmentally.

In counseling parents of adopted children, I have often found that there is commonly a gap in understanding—which is not to say that such a gap is never present with natural children. The adoptive parent is, however, relating to a child whose genetic makeup is unrelated to his own. Not only does the child lack a similar physical makeup (e.g., different features, different inborn susceptibilities), but he also has a different personality makeup. You and your husband may come from quiet and non-argumentative families, while your adopted child may come from a line of bellicose fighters. Or the reverse may be the case. The possibilities are endless. The point is that you may encounter styles of relating to life that are different from yours. You may not understand them and may have no idea how to respond to them. But these differences in temperament, though they complicate your relationship, should not be viewed judgmentally. There are many different ways of responding to our surroundings and to other people. And the ways we recognize as comfortable for us are not the only positive or useful ways.

I want to be very careful here to assure you that I am not condoning behaviors such as a child losing his temper. God's word is clear about what behaviors are pleasing to him, and unwarranted anger is not one of them. Nor do I want to suggest that anyone is locked into behaviors by his genetic makeup. You know how it goes, "Oh, I'm Irish, I can't help my temper." The Holy Spirit is capable of changing anyone into Christlikeness, and is in no way limited by inheritance. However, he does not wish to eradicate our own individual style. We are each unique, and that uniqueness is God-given. Your adopted child should not be just like you, nor like your natural child if you have one. Your natural child is not totally like you either, but there are "pieces" of you that seem recognizable. That was why it was easier for Marti to feel more at home with her natural daughter's personality and her way of relating to the world.

Perhaps the following example will illustrate the point. A Caucasian family adopted a little black boy, and when he was about four years old, his mother found him in the bathroom desperately trying to wash the black off his skin. He was aware of but did not understand the difference and wanted to eradicate it. The same dynamic may be present, but in reverse, for you and your adoptive child in regard to his personality. You are both aware that his is different, are uncomfortable with it, and perhaps want to make it go away. But if you, as the parent, were to "wash away" some of this difference, your child would lose some of his own essence, just as the little black boy would have if he had been able to change his color.

Marti's daughter carried her discomfort with difference even further, and felt that if she could not be "like" Marti, then she would be as different as possible—*must* be as different as possible—in order to find her "real" self. Marti's response to this defiant stance could have driven her daughter further away from her and the values she held dear. Instead, she sought counseling for the family. Marti came to understand she did not have to completely understand this child; none of us ever completely understands someone else. However, it was important that Marti's child be aware that her mother wanted to understand her, and to see Marti continually working at it. It was also important that Marti admit honestly when she was unable to.

The third concern here is the obsession that adopted children often develop with finding their natural parents. This is not uncommon, nor is it uncommon for adoptive parents to feel rejected by this pursuit. Perhaps it will help you understand your child better if you consider how insecure any child might feel if he thought his biological parents "gave him away." This a very difficult thing for a child to understand and it causes him great fear. Not that he doubts or rejects your love, but the fact that you love him does not eradicate what happened. The big question for the child is why? This often propels adopted children to search for the answer.

All human beings struggle with feelings of loneliness and emptiness. These can be especially prevalent during adolescence. Those of us with a bit more life experience know that such feelings are the nature of life in this world. Those who are younger and less mature still think that, if they can just do something (find their natural mother or father, find the right spouse, have the right job), these feelings of insecurity will go away. Nothing will alter those expectations except maturity. Remember also that one of the tasks of adolescence is finding identity. It was natural and appropriate that Marti's daughter desired to know more about her roots.

Obviously, this raises the question of whether or not you should allow or assist your child in this pursuit. I cannot answer that for you. The decision to keep the knowledge of natural parents hidden from a child may have been decided legally at the time of the adoption. If that is so, then you will have to help your child deal with the anger and the reality of facing the rest of his life with unanswered questions.

However, if that is not the case, then you will need great wisdom, and probably outside assistance in making that decision. Your child's personality, age, the wishes of his natural parents, and many other factors need to be considered. Clearly, you can only control whether a child will follow your wishes on this while he or she is under your care. When a child reaches adulthood he or she may choose to go against your advice.

That very real possibility brings us to another concern—the fear of losing your child, as Marti had when her daughter expressed a desire to know her birth parents. There is fear your wishes will be disregarded, that your love will be rejected. Those indeed are possibilities. However, those are possibilities with a natural child as well. No guarantees come with parenting. We are not promised that our children will accept us or our love for them, or that they will maintain a good relationship with us. There are great risks in parenting and there is nothing you can do to guarantee that you and your children will end up with wonderful, supportive relationships. Although you cannot control the outcome, you can make good relationships more likely by the way that you act. Every parent comes to the moment of letting a child go. Some sooner than later. When that time comes we need to let go in a way that keeps our door open. If they choose to return, they will do so as adults. That is what we all long for and work for during the growing-up years.

I hope you will learn to accept and even love the ways in which your child is different from you. I also hope that as you weather adolescence, you will do it in a way that allows for conflict without condoning destructive behavior. If you do lose your child for a time, keep the door open, and welcome him or her back with grace. In reality, your child is not yours and never was. Your child belongs to God and has been lent to you for a season.

TWENTY-FIVE

The Kids Are Gone and I Feel Empty

W HAT HAPPENS TO THE MOTHER who devotes twenty or thirty years to raising children and suddenly realizes her success has brought her much pain? The proof of her success is that her children are healthy, independent adults who no longer need her. And that, of course, is the paradox. The very thing she set out to achieve is now the cause of her feelings of emptiness and worthlessness. She loved those years, she misses her children terribly, and she feels she has nothing to look forward to that approaches the joy she found in mothering.

These feelings of sadness and loss, of a life that seems empty and meaningless, are often called the empty nest syndrome. It shouldn't be surprising that the woman who has spent more than half her life in an emotionally demanding role, requiring tremendous investments of time and energy, would suffer from such an adjustment.

If you find yourself in an empty nest, it is important that you recognize the legitimacy of your feelings, and not think that there is something wrong with you. Any major life change, good or bad, requires a period of adjustment and causes some degree of stress. The empty nest syndrome is not only a major change, but one that is often viewed negatively. Two questions loom ahead: How do I deal with my grief and loss? and, What do I do now?

Death always brings a sense of grief and loss. It is important to realize that you are facing the death of an era. A way of life that existed for you for perhaps twenty or thirty years is now over. It is natural to want to deny your loss and to resent it, as well as to feel depressed. These are normal grief reactions, and although you certainly wouldn't want to get stuck in this phase, or allow its negativity to control the rest of your life, you also need to remember that working through it will take some time. Give yourself that time and don't berate yourself for your struggle with this adjustment.

An essential you may lose sight of is that you still need to be there for your husband, or for other family members or friends. Your husband also has his own adjustment to make. His may not be so obvious, but it is real nonetheless. He is also having to adjust to living with a sad and struggling wife. In dealing with your feelings, don't communicate to him that to be left with "just him" is somehow bad or inadequate. It would be natural for him to feel rejected if you were to do that. On the contrary, his importance in your life is not diminished, it has become even more important. However, it is true that he cannot fill the void left by your grown children.

It is equally important that you not burden your children with responsibility for the quality of your life. If you are not careful you will communicate to them a resentment of the growth you worked so hard to accomplish! They have done what you brought them up to do—grown up and developed lives of their own. They will certainly continue to be a part of your life and your husband's, but how they do that will be very different from the days when they were at home and in school. And that is as it should be. It is fine to let them know that you are grappling with the sadness their leaving has caused you. But it is not good to suggest that it is up to them to make that sadness go away. To suggest it is their responsibility will injure your relationships with them.

You may believe that since you have done nothing but be a wife and mother, you're not good at anything else. I strongly urge you to question that! Of all the jobs on this planet, mothering is one of the most multifaceted I can think of. In your many years of mothering you have performed an incredible variety of tasks, some simple, but some also very complex. You have worked with your hands, you have mediated quarrels and orchestrated schedules. The list is probably endless. To say you have "done nothing but..." is a gross understatement!

Look back over all those years. Which tasks did you love? Which did you hate? About which were you indifferent? Where do your strengths lie? You can sort through your answers and find any number of things which you found particularly satisfying and which you are good at. And we haven't even mentioned church or community involvement, responsibilities you couldn't have escaped while raising children! Someone along the way snared you into their service, I'm sure! Which of those activities made you happy and confident? Which brought you the positive feedback we all need? Each answer is a piece of the puzzle you can put together to make a picture of yourself.

The empty nest period is marked by lack of motivation. But that will return in time. You are a woman who is used to a full and productive life, and must trust that eventually you will desire to have that again. As that motivation grows, go back over your life as I have suggested and also get input from others. Slowly you will begin to shape your future. Worthless you are not. You are a woman gifted by God, whose life is full of rich possibilities. I hardly think he will let them go to waste. For example, you have much to offer to young women struggling with marriage and motherhood. You have much wisdom and experience to offer children, for you have certainly had practice in relating to them. Somehow the pieces will come together and a new avenue, or many, will open up for you.

There is one more concern to consider at this point, and that is not to let yourself be locked into thinking you "have" to find a career. Should you decide to go back to school or in some other way pursue a career, that is fine. But there are many outlets for you other than formal work. Modern society tells women—men, too—that unless what they are doing requires a college degree or two, and can be called a career, it is not worthwhile nor will it be fulfilling.

If that's so, then Christ's life was not worthwhile or fulfilling! You can be sure God will help you tap into the many years he has brought you through, to use them in a productive way. One clear possibility is for you to find active ways to encourage young mothers, whose own mothers are not nearby. Your years of experience, combined with loving affirmation, could meet a tremendous need in their lives.

Our God is not a wasteful God. Whatever you decide to do, you can be sure it will make use of the gifts he has given you. As you remain open to his leading, you can be certain that your empty nest will once again be a place of success and personal fulfillment.

TWENTY-SIX

My In-Laws Criticize My Husband Constantly

Tom and Melissia live in the same small town as Tom's parents. Both Tom's mother and father are extremely critical of Tom. They criticize his job, his house, his clothes, and everything else about him. Melissia sometimes wonders if "everything" includes her.

Tom is an only child and his parents are elderly, so he feels obligated to run by their house daily "just to make sure they are okay." In doing this, he subjects himself to constant criticism. Melissia often feels angry and frustrated. She loves Tom, respects him, and wants very much to encourage him. She often finds herself criticizing her in-laws in return, with the result that Tom retreats into silence.

It is very hard to see the man you married criticized constantly by anyone. It is also very difficult to be comfortable with in-laws who treat your husband that way. Seeing your spouse always attacked as "not good enough," seeing his self-esteem shrink when he is in their company would make any wife angry. If this is the case with "your Tom," the odds of your being able to change it alone are pretty slim. A wiser approach I believe is to ask yourself, "How can I react in a way that is helpful to Tom and our kids?"

First, it is obvious that unlike your husband's parents, you will need to build him up rather than tear him down. It is important to have a realistic understanding of what that means. It would be very easy to feel that you are responsible to counteract all of your in-laws' negative comments. If you assume this responsibility, you will try each time he comes home from seeing them to find out what they said and how your husband feels about it. Then you will jump in with statements that attempt to negate theirs. It may be that only one of his parents makes him feel that he can never measure up. But whether it is the mother or the father, the effect is the same. You will want to respond with, *"Doesn't she realize she says you never..." "But doesn't he realize that you always..."*

The focus of such remarks is your mother or father-in-law, not your husband. You will, in reality, be arguing *against them*, rather than *for him*. You do indeed want to build him up, but not by trying to counteract them. There are two reasons for this. The first is that the negative input your husband gets from them hurts him because it is his *parents* who are attacking him. Nothing you say will make it as if they supported him; only they can do that. For example, if his mother says he is stupid, and you say he is smart, your husband will simply absorb that as two distinct opinions. Your feedback will not cancel out hers. He will still hear that his mother thinks he is stupid, and that will hurt. It is important for you to see this distinction; otherwise you will pit yourself against your in-laws. You need to throw your weight behind your husband, not because they are against him, but because you are for him.

The second reason it is important to understand this dynamic is to safeguard your own relationship with your in-laws. If you see yourself solely as in the position of counteracting their effects on their son's life, you will have nothing but a relationship of opposition. You and they will become enemies. I am sure there are times when you feel they are enemies. However, if that is how the relationship is structured your husband will be placed in a dilemma. He will feel he is the reason for a split, that he is the battleground on which you and his parents continually meet.

You have a tremendous challenge before you to nurture and respect your husband because of who he is, as well as to find ways to relate to both of your in-laws apart from their destructive actions toward him. If you do not work at this, they will become the center of your marriage—which may be what they unconsciously want to do, with their constant demands and criticisms of your husband. Love is central to the relationship between you and your mate, not a battle plan to counteract his parents.

Free your husband to work on his relationship with his parents as he sees fit. You, I am sure, would like nothing better than to tell them off and leave town. And it might be possible that moving would be a good thing for you both to do, especially if your situation is like one couple's I know. They lived five minutes from extremely critical in-laws and finally decided that the survival of the husband's self-esteem and their marriage dictated a move. However, growth in your husband will occur only as he faces the situation and makes decisions about how to respond to it. You cannot make him see what his parents are doing, nor can you make him choose a particular course of action, so the less you pit yourself against them the more freedom your husband will have to stand back and look at the effect they are having on his life. As long as you are the attacker of either of his parents, he will constantly feel obligated to defend them, and will not have the freedom to assess them critically.

Another effect of your disengaging in this way is that your own positive (and negative) input into your husband's life will have more impact. He will hear you as a person apart, not just write off your comments with, "Oh, she is just saying that because she knows Dad upset me." Both your praise and your suggestions will carry much more weight. You see, the question is not how to get rid of your in-laws and their impact on your husband, but rather how to nurture your marriage so that it is strong and good in spite of them.

Certainly this must be balanced with the realistic understanding that your husband does need to deal with his relationship with his parents. It would be wonderful if he would recognize how they hurt him and affect him and seek help in dealing with them. You can certainly suggest that, but you cannot force it. If you push trying to get him to change his relationship with his parents, you will be engaged in the same dynamic with him as they are, because you, too, will have become his critic. The fact that you see your efforts as an attempt to undo what they are doing, or that you use positive words to erase their negative ones, will not alter his perception that you, too, are judging him. To him, it will seem as if you are saying, "If you were more of a man, you wouldn't let your mother and father do this to you." He will feel stuck between two critical "teams" playing tug of war with him. He would likely respond by continuing to go to his parents', but just tell you less and less of what transpired while he was there.

I have one more practical suggestion. If your husband visits his folks regularly without you or your children, perhaps this could be changed somewhat. Maybe you could make more visits together, and have your calls be both short and structured to avoid some of the negative interaction. If you went along to catch them up on the children and their activities and accomplishments, or even took time alone to show them their work from school, or something of that nature, it might alleviate your husband's burden of keeping up his filial relationship alone. If you do this, you must go prepared for how you will respond to criticisms against your husband and yourself. If either parent speaks against your husband, do not allow yourself to be pulled into the discussion. You might simply smile and say something positive about him, and change the subject. You can respond the same way to a judgment, spoken or implied, against you or your children, for you cannot win. You will only lose and walk away angry. Instead, keep your talks informational and chatty, and most important, do not feel obligated to come up with a rebuttal for complaints.

You walk a difficult path. Your husband has a problem relationship with his parents which may never change. But ultimately, it is his to resolve. You must allow him the freedom to make his own choice in the matter. Unfortunately, he may choose never to face it and that will be exceedingly hard for you.

Your question is not how to get your husband to change, though indeed that would be for his good, but rather, "How am I to live to the glory of God with this man who may choose never to face a major problem in his life?"

Whenever anyone is in that dilemma, it is very easy to allow the focus to become the other person's refusal to face the problem. Whether your husband faces his or not, your responsibility is the same. You are called to respect and love him regardless of circumstances. Lovingly encourage him to seek help, but do not condemn him if he chooses not to do so. That will be very hard to accept if the outcome is that you must spend the years until his parents' death watching them hurt the man you love. It will require great discipline to continually redirect your focus from fighting them to loving him.

Part Four

A Woman and Her Psychology

TWENTY-SEVEN

Why Am I So Depressed?

D EPRESSION IS THIS NATION'S number one mental illness. The National Institute of Mental Health reports that 125 thousand Americans are hospitalized annually with depression, and another 200 thousand or more are treated by mental health professionals. All of us are susceptible to depression. No position in life makes us exempt for depression is no respecter of persons. The pervasiveness of depression and its debilitating effects make it important for us to think about.

First, I would like to differentiate between two kinds of depression: one is severe (sometimes referred to as "clinical," "significant," or "major" depression); the other is relatively mild. All of us are subject to periodic cases of "the blues" which can last for several days. Often, these periods of unhappiness are a reaction to disappointment or loss. We feel sad, forlorn, and sometimes listless. In severe depressions, however, the sadness becomes protracted (i.e., over two weeks) and may be characterized by the following: loss of interest or pleasure, changes in appetite with weight loss or gain, sleep disturbance (often waking too early, feeling unrefreshed—sometimes "hypersomnia," or too much sleep), feeling of agitation or low energy, problems with concentration, or pervasive feelings of guilt with recurrent thoughts of death or suicide. Significant depression also can be covered up, or "masked," by physical symptoms such as gastrointestinal complaints or anxiety. This pattern may be especially true in children. In adolescents, extended negative or antisocial behavior, combined with unusual sulkiness or social withdrawal, are prevalent. In the elderly, depression may manifest itself in listlessness and cognitive impairment, which may be confused with dementia.

When depressions are severe, treatment with antidepressant medications, as well as counseling, are necessary. Antidepressant drugs should not be confused with minor tranquilizers or sedatives, which work almost immediately and can be addictive. One doesn't get "hooked" on antidepressants, nor do they make one "high" or happy. Rather, these medications generally take at least two weeks to begin working and usually need to be taken over the course of months, even well after the symptoms of depression have abated. Your family physician may prescribe these medications, or he or she may refer you to a psychiatrist for antidepressants, especially when a depression is resistant to treatment.

Many people suffer from depression because of a predisposition to depressive illness. This disorder is not necessarily caused by difficulties with living, spiritual problems, or lack of faith. Severe, biological depressions can happen through no fault of one's own, and need to be treated like any other medical illness.

What are some other possible sources of depression? First, and often ignored, is personality type. Some people, by temperament, are more prone to feeling nervous, frightened, or apprehensive. Each of us is unique, with our own characteristics, weaknesses, and failures. Some of us live with a self that is extroverted and self-assured. Others of us live with a self that is fearful, introspective, and prone to depression. We each need to get to know and understand ourselves. I think Christians often make the mistake of assuming that all Christians are identical with respect to personality. Personality makes no difference in our salvation, but it can make a very great difference in our actual experience of the Christian life.

A second possible cause for feelings of depression and anxiety can be our physical condition. Just imagine the despair of the woman in Mark 5 who had had an "issue of blood" for twelve years, had made endless trips to physicians, depleted her finances, and kept getting worse! We cannot isolate the emotional from the physical, for body and mind are interdependent. Hypoglycemia, thyroid imbalance, hormonal changes, different kinds of poisoning, and drug side effects are all physical considerations in diagnosing depression. Fatigue, poor eating and sleeping habits, and stress-filled lives also provide fertile ground for emotional difficulties.

A third possible cause of depression is that it is simply a reaction to trauma. The accomplishment of an important goal, an illness, a tragedy such as death, divorce, or infidelity, difficult circumstances such as severe loneliness—all can bring on depression.

There are events peculiar to women which can bring on depression—a letdown following marriage, the birth of a child, the last child going to school or leaving home, and infertility. Women who isolate themselves from others and who have no social or intellectual outlet other than home and family, often become filled with anger as their husbands find fulfillment in careers and outside interests. This anger frequently goes unexpressed and results in depression.

For such a woman, the adjustment to adult children leaving home can be devastating, especially if coupled with emotional difficulties precipitated by menopause. These very real crises can become excuses, unless the woman makes the critical decision to accept responsibility for her life. She can better do this if she plants her stability and self-esteem in the unchanging love and provision of Christ, rather than in fallible circumstances and people.

A final cause of depression is in the spiritual area. Just as we cannot separate body from mind, so we cannot separate either from the spirit. Although each of these is a separate entity, a dysfunction in one frequently affects the other. If, as a Christian, I cease to be obedient to the Word of God, then I am out of fellowship with him. This division in my relationship with God leaves the door open for spiritual depression, because God is not free to fill me with his peace. Until that time when I confess my sin and return to walking in obedience to him, I will be beleaguered with doubts and guilt, resulting in a spiritually depressed state.

There are Christians who will not admit to depression. They say that a Christian is one who has joy all the time, and that this has always been true for them. But the truth is, no life is always wonderful, and reality is often harsh. People hurt Christians; tragedies occur to Christians. Scripture is kind to such Christians. If they become depressed, Scripture does not condone their depression or indulge it, but it does recognize the fact of its existence and suggests ways of handling such times in our lives.

The key to handling much depression lies, I think, in how we handle our feelings. What is the place of feelings in the Christian life? The trend today is, of course, an overemphasis on feelings. People make decisions based on feelings alone. Emotions control their lives. Christianity does not commend that. It gives priority to the mind. However, that priority is balanced by a regard for feelings. Christianity recognizes that emotions are vital to being human. We are told that God does not despise our tears, but rather takes special note of them by recording them in his book (Psalm 56:8).

Two characteristics of feelings are simple but vital. First, we cannot command our feelings at will. We are, in this area, not masters of ourselves. You can tell yourself over and over not to feel something, but that generally has no effect whatsoever. Second, feelings are changeable. They depend on many factors, and can change quickly. Nothing is so surprising as going to bed happy, and then upon waking, finding yourself in a completely different mood.

Because of our inability to command our feelings, and because of their variability, it is important that we do not allow them to control us. This is especially important to those whose personalities make them prone to fearfulness and depression. Such people need less of a stimulus to produce a negative state of mind. The person who is naturally given to introspection and despair must realize that just because he knows Christ, his basic personality is not automatically changed. We vary in our weaknesses as well as our gifts.

Neither is temperament to control us. Unfortunately, some of us take great pride in allowing just that. We say, "Well, that's just the way I am." Temperament, personality, and feelings are gifts from God, but as a result of the Fall they are misused. Moods descend on us uninvited. We may go through the day in one mood until something happens to bring on another. Thus, we allow our feelings to rule our lives.

How then, are we to deal with feelings that are both variable and not at our command? First, make certain that there is no obvious cause for your absence of joy. If there is a spiritual problem—if you are harboring resentment, anger, or a critical spirit toward someone—then you will be depressed. Confess it and receive God's forgiveness. You cannot violate God's laws and experience joy.

Second, do not make feelings central. That is in direct opposition to today's thinking and may sound strange to some. The purpose of Scripture is not to stimulate us emotionally. Its primary purpose is to get us into a right relationship with God. Scripture is truth, and truth is addressed to the mind. Feelings can enhance or detract from our experience of truth, but they are not to control truth. For example, James 2:9 says, "But if you show partiality, you are committing sin and are convicted by the law as transgressors." That is a statement of truth, and a pretty clear one, I think. Yet how often we are governed by our feelings toward people, and hence show partiality! If a well-known person appears in church one Sunday alongside a drifter from the street, to whom do we extend a welcome? We show partiality based on our feelings toward the one who is a public figure, don't we? However, by God's grace, we can set aside our feelings and welcome both equally. This obviously carries over into many areas of our lives.

Depressed persons are often dependent, nonverbal, pessimistic, and poorly motivated. Because of those characteristics, intervention from another person is usually helpful in learning the cause of the depression, as well as ways to conquer it.

Sarah, a forty-seven-year-old mother of three, came for counseling, after struggling with depression for many years. As we considered her history and current circumstances, Sarah came to understand that her depression was rooted in her fear of motherhood. Her own mother had been both alcoholic and abusive. Sarah had determined not to be like her and had pursued a successful teaching career in a university, deliberately avoiding marriage and motherhood. In her thirties, however, she fell in love and married. Her husband very much wanted children, and she did not want to disappoint him. She pushed her fears away, determined to be a competent mother. They had three lovely children and Sarah became increasingly depressed.

Dealing with her depression was painful for Sarah, because it required facing painful memories of growing up. It also required forgiving her mother and learning that she was not who her mother said she was, nor did she have to be like her mother. As her depression lifted, Sarah was able to reach out to her children with love, rather than retreat from them in fear.

It is important to remember that all depression is not the same, anymore than all people are the same. We need to respond to those who are depressed with great gentleness. If the symptoms of a clinical depression are present, we need to guide them lovingly to professional help. Whether a depression is mild or severe, we need to remind ourselves, and others as they are able, to hear the words of Psalm 46:1-2: "God is our refuge and strength, a very present help in trouble. Therefore we will not fear, though the earth should change..."

TWENTY-EIGHT

How Should I Look at Myself?

I T IS NOT UNCOMMON FOR WOMEN struggling with low self-esteem to come to my office. Many are battling negative thoughts about themselves almost constantly, which inhibits them in their relationships with others, in their jobs, and in their ability to accept success. They may be uncertain and puzzled about how they should regard self-esteem as Christians.

A long history in the Western world of negative views about women and their worth is a major factor. Women have been put down by male authority figures such as Alexander Pope who made this incredulous statement: "Most women have no characters at all." Or, even the venerated, benevolent St. Augustine: "The woman herself alone is not the image of God: Whereas the man alone is the image of God as fully and completely as when the woman is joined with him." Men such as these have done much to shape thought about women through the ages.

Self-esteem is also a sensitive topic for women because of their relational nature. It is by the care and concern they show for others that women have judged their value and been judged by others. Women have been regarded according to the degree of their love, service, and self-sacrifice. An exceptional woman is often defined as one who immerses herself in the lives of others, making no demands on them and expecting no returns. Whenever women have been unable to make those around them happy or prevent them from being hurt, they stamp themselves—or are stamped by others—with low self-esteem.

You only have to walk into your local bookstore to know that self-esteem is a popular topic today. It concerns secular and Christian authors, who give varying messages. Scripture does not use the terms self-esteem or self-image, but it does give us guidance regarding how we are to consider ourselves. Oftentimes, scriptural counsel seems in direct opposition to popular thought. For example, how do you reconcile such statements as, "When I love you more than I love myself, I am really loving you less," with "He who loves his life loses it"? Or, "It is an established fact that nobody is born with the ability to love himself," against "For no man ever hated his own flesh, but nourishes it and cherishes it"? How do you mesh, "The act of self-acceptance is the root of all things," with "This is the first and greatest commandment, Thou shalt love the Lord your God with all your heart, soul, and mind"?

Puzzling, isn't it? Both views cannot be right. Yet Christians try to hold both. This is evident in the fact that the above statements (except those which are from Scripture) all come from Christian authors!

How am I to think about myself? Should I work at loving myself, or at hating myself? Am I important, or am I nothing? What is self-esteem in a proper, scriptural sense?

How about starting where Christ himself started? He began with what he called the first and greatest commandment, the root of all things: "You shall love the Lord your God with all your heart, and with all your soul, and with all your mind" (Matthew 22:37). Christ gave this command preeminence because our relationship with the Creator God is the basis for all existence. Man and his relationship to himself is not central, and those who make this assumption are in error, no matter how "right" they sound or how good their words make us feel when we act upon them.

God is the beginning from which we start. We are commanded first and foremost to love him with everything we have. Nowhere in Scripture are we told that this is predicated on a healthy self-love. God is central, not man or anything he might be, do, or possess.

We often hear that women whose fathers were abusive cannot love God until their self-image is positive, or until they learn to love themselves. I believe that this is backwards. Women will not truly have proper self-esteem until they know God and experience who he is. I have known many women whose self-esteem was off the charts negatively due to horrible abuse as children, yet they have loved God with all their hearts. There may have been much about God the Father they did not understand and they sometimes feared him unnecessarily. But they loved him and obeyed him. As their relationship with him matured, their self-esteem rose significantly.

If you bring your energies to bear on learning to know and love God, two things will happen. First, the way you think about everything, including yourself, will be changed. And second, your love for God will be evident.

Before Scripture has barely unfolded, God tells us that we are made in his image (Genesis 1:27). When you hear someone comment that a boy is "just the image" of his father, you are being told that he looks like his father. God has told us that we were made to look like *him*. He has said that "we are fearfully and wonderfully made" (Psalm 139). "We are His workmanship, created in Christ Jesus" (Ephesians 2:10). God has, in essence, said that who you are is significant. This is an eternal truth of God, regardless of whether you are tall or short, fat or thin, loved or unloved by others. This truth does not depend on appearance, behavior, or experience.

God's next verse tells us we are to be workers and fruit-bearers (Genesis 1:28). Not only is who we *are* significant, but also what we do. God has made us in his image and we are to have an impact upon his world. We are to care for his world and be fruitful in it. Both are reflections of who he is. Our actions matter and affect the rest of his creation. Again, this is not rooted in whether or not we feel significant and important, but rather in God's word about us. We may feel useless and inconsequential, of no value to God or others, but how God views us does not depend on how we view ourselves with our own eyes.

The third thing God says about his fallen creatures is that our reflection of his image is distorted, marred. We are like children who once looked like their father, but due to an accident their faces are scarred. Flickers of the resemblance remain, but the likeness has been distorted. Jeremiah 17:9 says, "The heart is more deceitful than all else and is desperately sick; who can understand it?" God says very early in Genesis (8:21) that "the intent of man's heart is evil." Who we are and what we do remains significant, but now we cannot trust that how we think, what we do, or how we feel is in keeping with God and his word.

One of the results of this sinfulness is that we have a wrong view of ourselves. Rather than keeping God central, man has put himself in the center. This can be shown in opposite ways. Some of us have made ourselves central by investing all our energies into thinking how *important* we are. We are proud and arrogant and are devoted to caring for ourselves at the expense of others. Others of us have made ourselves central by investing our energies in *hating* ourselves. We treat ourselves in ways that are unfounded. Our minds are continually focused on how bad, unimportant, and worthless we are. Both extremes are wrong, yet one or the other may be constantly pulling us in its direction. How are we to find a balance?

God continued to demonstrate how much he valued us by sending Christ to die for us. Though our hearts are deceitful and devise evil continually, we can be redeemed in Christ.

God has intervened so as to again make us look like him. Paul says in 2 Corinthians 3:18, "But we all, with unveiled face beholding as in a mirror the glory of the Lord, are being transformed into the same image." This transformation is not instantaneous; it is a process. The distortions and marring are still very real. I must live with them on a daily basis because the effects of sin run deep. At the same time, I am being made over to look like Jesus. Who I am continues to be significant to God, whether it is to mankind or not. What God does through me has significant impact on others, whether I know it does or not.

It is important that we understand that our reshaping and redefining continues lifelong. Growth for some of us is stunted because of wrong teaching about God, abuse by our parents, or hurtful behavior by others. Any woman who grew up with physical, verbal, or sexual abuse will take a long time to grasp the worth God places upon her life. To tell such a woman she is of value to God will seem almost nonsensical, for she has never been told she is of value to anyone. Obviously, that indicates the importance of patient love for others. Our treatment of another human being as valuable, may help her begin taking steps along the road of understanding who she is in Christ.

God's teaching about who we are enables us to think of ourselves realistically. Romans 12:3 says we are "… not to think more highly of himself than he ought to think; but to think so as to have sound judgment…" We are to recognize both our worth and lack of it. In grasping that, our significance is rooted in God himself, we will see the importance of our lives and our actions. We will see that we have impact on others, that we can positively affect their growth, their understanding of God, and their choices. In grasping our sinfulness, we will see the importance of humility, for we will understand that we are utterly dependent upon God, that our hearts can deceive us again and again, that we can manipulate and hurt others and use our God-given strength to dishonor the very One who gave it to us.

Thus we will find balance in the way we think about ourselves and live our lives. Our acceptance by God in Christ is complete because it was bought and paid for in full at his cross. No life experience, no emotional trauma can take that acceptance away. Life may cloud our awareness of it, experiences may hamper our belief in it, but it is ours regardless.

Having accepted and esteemed us at great cost, God in Christ has now called us to live out our lives so that we look like him. At last we are at one with God's purpose when he created the first man and woman; "But we have this treasure in earthen vessels, that the surpassing greatness of the power may be of God and not from ourselves.... that the life of Jesus also may be manifested in our mortal flesh" (2 Corinthians 4:7, 11).

We carry a great treasure within us. Whatever our gifts, however large or small our circle of influence, whatever our position and power, we carry the treasure of Christ himself within us. We bear that treasure in an earthen vessel. It is a marred vessel, a suffering vessel, a weak and deceitful vessel. We have to work hard not to forget our significance, especially when the world seems to scream at us that we are worthless or no good. We are the daughters of a King.

We will also have to work hard not to forget our sinfulness, especially when success and the praise of others clouds our awareness of it. We are of the dust. We are to walk with confidence, as well as with humility. Why? So that we may know the surpassing greatness of the power of God.

C.S. Lewis captured the balance we seek in his book *Prince Caspian;* "You come of the Lord Adam and the Lady Eve, and that is both honor enough to lift up the head of the poorest beggar, and shame enough to bow the shoulders of the greatest emperor on earth."

We can maintain a critical balance between the honor and the shame of who we are, if we continually seek to love the Lord our God with all our hearts. Only then, of course, does who we are bring glory to his name.

TWENTY-NINE

I Live with Panic

T ANYA CAME TO SEE ME SEVERAL YEARS AGO afraid she could no longer care for her two children. She complained of episodes of dizziness, shortness of breath, chest pains, heart palpitations, and uncontrollable trembling. During these times the world seemed distant and unreal, and she feared she was going crazy or completely losing control. She had seen her doctor who reported after a thorough exam that she was physically healthy. It was he who suggested that she come to see me.

Tanya had dropped out of all her activities in church and her children's schools. She was terrified of going to the grocery store. Crowds, and particularly elevators, frightened her. Driving brought great anxiety. It was all she could do to get herself to my office. She had begged her husband to hire a nanny or let her mother come to stay with them, for she was sure that if something happened to one of the children she would be helpless.

Tanya was suffering from a psychological disorder known as panic attacks. This dysfunction is marked by sudden, overwhelming, seemingly irrational terror, and is accompanied by at least several of the following symptoms: sweating, heart palpitations, hot or cold flashes, trembling, feelings of unreality, a choking sensation, shortness of breath, chest discomfort, faintness, dizziness, and fears of dying, losing control, or going crazy. Often, the sufferer of a first panic attack rushes to the hospital, certain that she is having a heart attack. The occurrence of attacks is unpredictable, although certain situations, such as elevators, can become associated with them. If not treated, panic sufferers can become increasingly avoidant or "agoraphobic" to the extent that venturing outside their homes can be difficult.

Panic attacks occur predominantly in women. They usually have their onset between the ages of seventeen and thirty. The disorder is estimated to affect over one million Americans. After several attacks, the victim may develop what is called "anticipatory" anxiety, which is often as disabling as the panic attacks themselves. The anticipation of an attack leads the victims to avoid more and more of the places associated with the onset of the dreaded feelings. They may avoid bridges, tunnels, crowded rooms, elevators, stores, restaurants, and other enclosed places. The effect can be crippling, causing the person to become suffocatingly dependent on her spouse, a relative, a friend—or anyone whose presence alleviates the fear. Needless to say this dependence can be exhausting and frustrating for those who try to help.

Much evidence indicates panic disorder is both biologically and psychologically different from ordinary anxiety. The first attack is usually spontaneous and the symptoms almost entirely physical. Attacks seem to come and go with no relation to particular events, but often first occur after a period of stress. Heredity appears to be a factor. The rate of the disorder among families of persons experiencing panic attacks may be as high as fifteen to twenty percent. Although there are many theories regarding the cause, attacks are probably not the result of any single situation or condition. Instead, physical and environmental aspects likely combine to create the condition.

Many different approaches exist in the treatment of panic disorder. Some mental health professionals emphasize buried or repressed feelings, the consequence of which is anxiety. Other therapists concentrate on family relationships and the role that anxiety plays in these. Behavioral treatment may include relaxation training, biofeedback, and gradual exposure to dreaded situations. Many self-help groups draw upon these techniques. Treatment which combines medication and psychotherapy can be very effective. Antidepressant drugs have been found to be helpful in preventing the attacks themselves. Improvement with the use of antidepressants usually can be seen after about the third week. Tranquilizers are sometimes used initially because they act immediately.

Women experiencing panic attacks need encouragement, reassurance, empathy, advice, and explanations of their illness. While they should not be overprotected, their fears should not be belittled. Those suffering panic attacks should gain comfort from the fact that even in the most severe cases, the outlook is optimistic. Studies have shown that, while taking medication, seventy percent of patients improve.

Tanya found initial relief in medication. She then felt able to face the truths the disorder would teach her. Tanya was overwhelmed by the responsibilities in her life and afraid that she would fail to meet them. She preferred dependency, helplessness, and passivity, all of which required others to rescue her. As she gradually faced her fears, her confidence grew along with her ability to function once again.

If you or someone you know has panic responses, first make certain that physical problems are not causing the symptoms. A host of medical conditions can cause or contribute to anxiety. Check those out. In addition, excess coffee, tea, and other caffeinated beverages can produce anxiety. Look at sleep habits. How about fatigue? It can fray the nerves.

A reminder; the history of those experiencing panic attacks usually reveals that initial symptoms have followed a period of stress. Interpersonal and marital conflicts, births, miscarriages, menopause, and gynecological surgery often precede the first attack.

Here are some practical suggestions that may help you cope if you are subject to panic. Remind yourself that the feelings are nothing more than an exaggeration of normal bodily reactions to stress. They are not harmful or dangerous—although they are unpleasant. Nothing worse will happen.

Second, try not to add to the panic with frightening thoughts about what is happening and where it might lead.

Third, pay attention to what is actually happening in your body right then, not what you fear *might* happen.

Finally, give yourself time for the fear to pass. Try not to fight it or run away from it, but just accept it. Notice that when you stop adding to the fear with frightening thoughts, the fear starts to fade by itself. Remember that every time you face the fear without running from it, you've made progress and have learned more about how to cope more effectively.

Many women have found it helpful to write these steps out on a card that they can carry with them. When they begin to feel their anxiety rise, they take it out and read it over and over. It is a concrete way to redirect your thoughts positively. As with many emotional disturbances, women often are afraid to admit their neediness and to seek help. The admission of a physical problem is greeted with much more support and understanding in the Christian community, than is the revealing of an emotional difficulty. We fear that by telling others we are overcome with anxiety, we will be met with judgment and glib responses. A superficial application, given in passing, of such verses as "God has not given us the spirit of fear..." often does more harm than good. It is certainly true that God has not given us fear. However, to hold that up as what ought to be, thereby condemning what is, simply adds unnecessary guilt to the already heavy load.

Human beings are so complex, and the interaction of body, mind, and emotion is barely understood. We need to remember that just hearing truth does not immediately result in change. We are creatures of time, and everything we do, including growth, takes place over time. We would be wise to respond with grace to these pleas for support and understanding.

If you are the one needing help, do not hesitate to look for it from those who know how to give. If you are not, do not hesitate to give to those who are fearful.

THIRTY

I Think I Have
an Eating Disorder

SOCIETY HAS A STAGGERING EFFECT on the attitudes women have about themselves and their bodies. It "programs" them to view body fat and food in a strongly emotional way. This outlook can have a deleterious effect on both their physical and psychological health. Concerns about weight are considered normal. At any given time, thirty percent of the women in this country are actively dieting.

Just what is a compulsive eater? A compulsive eater is someone whose life is controlled by her relationship with food. Eating has gained the power to define her sense of self.

The first of these eating disorders is anorexia, the name given to compulsive undereating. An anorexic is obsessed with not eating and has an unnatural fear of food. She has a consuming need to feel in control of her body. The bulimic, on the other hand, consumes enormous amounts of food at one time and follows these binges with purging, through vomiting, taking laxatives, or switching to a severely restricted diet until the next binge. Since the bulimic typically perceives her behavior as extremely shameful, her binging and purging are done secretly.

The significant thing about each of these eating disorders is that it becomes an overwhelming preoccupation, sapping energy from other pursuits as well as restricting the way other time is spent. The pursuit of control via extremes of eating dominates the person's life.

This aberrant behavior does not have a sudden onset, but develops out of what might be considered normal efforts at weight control. The difference is that with some individuals the concern for thinness runs amuck and becomes the outlet for hidden emotional and psychological disturbances of unknown origin.

How does society contribute? Femininity is usually defined in American culture as being fragile, thin, and small. Women are encouraged to defer, to define themselves via their relationships. This prods them to become preoccupied with taking care of others, to depend on others for approval and validation. The message seems to be that if a woman is kind enough, thin enough, pretty enough, somebody will love her and take care of her. Some women who internalize such cultural beliefs about thinness will tend to develop obsessions about food. "Thinness" is perceived as power.

As the changing metabolic rate of a young girl causes her body to develop curves, she may react with panic and diet severely to feel in control of her body and gain the approval of others. Thinness represents power and control, or to put it another way, power is achieved through body size. "If I am thin I will get my needs met."

What may cause her to opt for anorexia or bulimia? Many books today suggest various theories. Anorexics are often said to want to stay children, so they compulsively undereat to keep their bodies child-like. They unconsciously fear womanhood. Bulimics, on the other hand, are often described as carrying hidden childhood rage. The binging is said to be an attempt to stuff feelings down, while the purging is an expression of rage and self-hatred.

Mothers are usually seen as a key player in the development of these disorders. The mother-daughter relationship tends to be shaped by the social world in which the mother lives and it is she who will communicate the values she thinks her daughter must develop to be successful. The mother may even say, "If you want to be a success, if you want to be loved, if you want to get married, then you must be pretty and thin." Fathers often are fat-phobic, and may have teased their daughters about weight. Often they are not affirming about the daughter's femininity.

Women with eating disorders tend to feel worthless and powerless. They often have difficulty expressing their feelings, especially anger. Achieving intimacy is difficult, and they may have confused feelings about their sexuality. They almost always have a very distorted body image, with an inability to assess their weight realistically. Often they are achievers and perfectionists.

The eating disorder fulfills many functions for such women. It is sometimes a safe way to rebel against the societal and familial expectation of perfection which they have internalized. It is used as a coping mechanism for painful feelings, or as a way to express unacceptable anger. Sometimes it can develop in an attempt to bring parents together, for their concerns over their child's eating may become a point of agreement in an otherwise divided relationship. Or, it may be a way to perpetuate the pleasure the person felt when being taken care of as a child. Sometimes it serves as a way to abuse oneself. Clearly it is a very complex problem with biological, cultural, and psychological factors. To handle such a problem adequately in one chapter of a book is impossible.

Eating disorders that are detrimental to physical and emotional health are not self-treatable. Outside help is necessary. The first person to see is the family physician. Honesty regarding the person's history with food is essential. Both bulimia and anorexia can have severe consequences physically, and anyone who suffers from these ailments needs a thorough checkup. It is vital that no one enter any treatment program without medical oversight. The doctor will most likely recommend an inpatient or outpatient center and will confer with the patient about which seems better.

If you are the patient, part of your treatment will include developing new ways of thinking about yourself, your body, and food. If either the anorexia or bulimia is severe, hospitalization may be required. Some kind of food regimen will be instituted because normal weight restoration must occur if the psychological treatment is to be meaningful. Because thinking patterns, self-esteem issues, and developing autonomy are crucial concerns to both the anorexic and bulimic, therapeutic treatment may need to continue for several years. Simply achieving a normal weight does not mean the problem has been conquered. If the concerns which triggered the drive for thinness and instilled the fear of body fat are not resolved, the problem will simply recur.

A couple of closing thoughts are important for you as a Christian to understand. Hearing and even understanding them will not "fix" your problem, and they should not be taken as "the answer." They are simply thoughts to work through and mull over *while* you are actively involved in getting treatment.

The first is found in Romans 12:2, "And do not be conformed to this world, but be transformed by the renewing of your mind, that you may prove what the will of God is, that which is good and acceptable and perfect." That certainly means the society's values are not to shape us. It may also mean that those values implicit in our home as we grew up are equally not to control us.

Somewhere along the way you have picked up messages that have communicated to you that thinness is central. In buying into that message, you have been conformed to the world around you. You are, in Christ, free from worldly dictates. Enjoy that freedom!

Finally, from 1 Corinthians 6:19-20, "Or do you not know that your body is a temple of the Holy Spirit who is in you, whom you have from God, and that you are not your own? For you have been bought with a price: therefore glorify God in your body." You also are free to learn the power to take your body, which has been treated so destructively, and use it to glorify God himself. I urge you to see your doctor and begin!

THIRTY-ONE

Tell Me about Substance Abuse

MANY WOMEN WHOM I TREAT for addiction-related problems abuse alcohol. For others, it's prescription drugs. For both groups, what began as a means of controlling tension or pain eventually became life-controlling. The prison that addicted women find themselves in serves to shatter their beliefs about themselves and their ability to control their own lives. Their journey out of addiction requires taking a hard and honest look at themselves.

The use of mood-altering substances is, in many ways, accepted as normal in society today. Most of us drink coffee or tea for the stimulating effects of caffeine, and some consume alcohol socially. Many women use drugs to relieve tension or pain and or to suppress appetite. When the substance becomes harmful, substance use has become substance abuse.

Substance abuse, when defined as the misuse of alcohol, cigarettes, and both legal and illegal drugs, is easily the most significant cause of preventable illness, disability, and death in the United States today. About 25.5 million Americans are affected by alcohol and drug abuse. When we consider the effects on families and people close to the abusers, as well as those killed by intoxicated drivers, such abuse affects millions more.

Substance abuse victims cannot control their use of alcohol or other drugs. They become intoxicated regularly—perhaps daily or on weekends or binges. In time, they may need the drug daily to function. They may repeatedly attempt to stop, but fail. Victims of substance *dependence* suffer all the symptoms of abuse, but also develop a physical need and a tolerance for the substance so that increased amounts of the drug are necessary for the desired effect. This means that the person develops withdrawal symptoms when she stops using the drug.

Let's consider four kinds of addiction: Alcohol, prescription drugs, illegal drugs, and nicotine. We have long viewed alcohol abuse as a psychological problem which hooks only those who lack self-discipline or who are immoral. Needless to say, this perspective has silenced many alcoholics about their addiction. Recent scientific discoveries have begun to change this view. It now appears that, in some cases, predisposition to alcoholism can be biological and inherited. This finding offers hope and support for the victims of alcohol whose addiction may be attributed to physical predisposition—not to weak-will or immorality.

The hallmark of alcoholism (or any drug abuse) is denial. The abuse of alcohol is especially easy to deny, because the consumption of alcohol is socially acceptable. Many alcohol abusers maintain that they are not truly alcoholics because they are "not on skid row" or "can stop any time they want to." Often, they kid themselves into believing that true alcoholics drink hard liquor and that beer or wine is somehow more benign. (In fact, the amount of alcohol by volume in a serving of beer can be equivalent to a shot of hard liquor.)

Alcohol abuse comes in many forms. Habitual excessive drinking on weekends is no less serious than drinking every day. Drinking during the night is no more or less destructive than drinking during the day. It bears repeating that the chief defense against admitting a problem with alcohol is denial. Perhaps that is why the first step of Alcoholics Anonymous requires admitting one's powerlessness over alcohol.

Alcohol dependence can bring serious withdrawal symptoms such as restlessness, irritability, sweating, and nausea which may progress into delirium tremens (DT's) and seizures. Heavy drinking over a long period of time can cause a form of dementia which results in memory and thinking impairment. The physical complications of alcoholism include stomach problems, cirrhosis, hepatitis, and a host of other alcohol-related medical disorders. The children of women who use alcohol during pregnancy may show signs of fetal alcohol syndrome, with symptoms including low birth weight and mental retardation.

Approaches vary in the treatment of alcoholism. The self-help group Alcoholics Anonymous continues to be one of the most effective approaches to alcohol abuse. A related organization, Al-Anon, can be of tremendous help to the family of alcohol abusers. Individual and family counseling can be valuable in addressing the wide-ranging effects that result from alcohol abuse. At times, hospitalization is required for safe withdrawal from alcohol as well as for further treatment.

The abuse of prescription medications most frequently involves drugs which may be referred to as anxiolytics, minor tranquilizers, sedative hypnotics, or sleeping pills. Among these are benzodiazepines (Valium, Librium, Tranxene, Ativan, Xanax, etc.) and barbiturates (Amytal, Seconal, Nembutal, etc.). Two benzodiazepine drugs are marketed for sleep difficulties—Restoril and Halcion.

Xanax has become a widely-prescribed benzodiazepine class drug which may have especially severe withdrawal effects if not taken and discontinued according to instructions. Smaller amounts of Xanax are equivalent to higher dosages of similar medications. More recently, an antianxiety medication called BuSpar has been marketed on the basis of producing no significant sedation or tolerance and is thus more readily prescribed by many physicians.

When sedatives or anxiolytics are taken to promote sleep, a rebound of anxiety or sleep difficulties, or both, may ensue when the drug is discontinued. This is especially an issue when barbiturates are used to facilitate sleep, as these medications can alter the quality of sleep and cause nightmares if discontinued suddenly. Sleep aids can also become habit forming by virtue of a "psychological dependence" that develops when the user becomes accustomed to the sedative effects of these drugs and is unable to sleep without them. It is important to remember that, unless the problems which underlie anxiety or sleeplessness are resolved, the symptoms are likely to reemerge when the drug is discontinued.

This is *not* to say that anxiolytics and sleeping pills should never be taken. These medications can be tremendously helpful during periods in which we feel overwhelmed by anxiety or insomnia. Taking a judiciously prescribed medication does not necessarily mean that the patient will become addicted. Reliance on these medications over time can be fraught with problems, however, and thus requires vigilance on the part of both doctor and patient.

The third area which we need to consider briefly is that of illegal drug use, which ranges from the inhalation of solvents (glue, paint thinners, etc.) to the use of "designer drugs." We will be able to touch upon only a few of these in this chapter.

Cocaine is a stimulant drug which can be inhaled, injected, or smoked. It causes a rapid euphoric effect that leads to an intense craving for more of the drug. Anyone who tries cocaine or "crack" (a form of cocaine that is chemically altered so it can be smoked) risks addiction. Dependency on this drug is so powerful that it comes to rule every part of the user's life.

Marijuana is the most widespread and frequently used

illicit drug in this country. The health consequences of marijuana use depend on the frequency, duration, and intensity of use, and the age at which the use begins. Adverse reactions to marijuana can include panic reactions, disorientation, flashbacks, and amotivational syndrome, a chronic pattern of apathy and poor judgment.

Hallucinogens (such as LSD, mescaline, and peyote) are taken orally and can cause the abuser to experience hallucinations and a sense of insight. Most people are introduced to these drugs by experimenting with them in social situations. Adverse reactions to hallucinogens include acute panic and psychosis.

Other commonly abused drugs include the opioids (e.g., morphine and its derivatives: Heroin, Delaudid, Percodan, etc.). When prescribed medically, these drugs can ease pain and suffering. Because they also produce a sense of euphoria and tranquility, however, the opioids are widely abused and sold illegally.

The amphetamines are a stimulant drug which have a number of legitimate medical uses but which are also frequently manufactured and sold illegally. Amphetamines can produce wakefulness, elevated mood and confidence, as well as diminished appetite. Many chronic amphetamine abusers first begin taking these drugs for weight loss or to fight fatigue. Tolerance to the drug results in increased use and abuse.

The final aspect of substance abuse that we will consider is nicotine addiction. The United States Surgeon General's latest report confirmed that nicotine in tobacco products is an addictive drug comparable to heroin or morphine. Close to 50 million Americans smoke cigarettes, and 320 thousand deaths a year result from the use of tobacco products. Smokers become addicted to the mood-altering, stress-reducing properties of nicotine. Nicotine acts on specific receptors in the brain and other parts of the nervous system.

It also relaxes the skeletal muscles and may suppress appetite. Withdrawal symptoms from nicotine can include craving for the drug, irritability, anger, anxiety, difficulty concentrating, and weight gain. The constant presence of other smokers, the easy availability of cigarettes, and the frequent reminders of advertisers make quitting extremely difficult—even without the added pressure of physical dependence.

An honest admission of addiction is the first step to conquering it. If those close to you are registering concern about your consumption of any of the above-mentioned substances, stop and listen. The odds are that they see you more clearly than you see yourself. The second step, also a difficult one, is to seek help. Recognizing and admitting an addiction is often followed by the belief that we can conquer the problem without help. This is not likely. Those who are addicted generally need long-term support. They need insight into their behavior patterns and motivation. They need help in developing higher self-esteem, as well as in learning new ways of coping with stress. Seeking help can be especially hard for Christians, because they are aware of the sad fact that the church sometimes shoots its wounded. We Christians are frequently afraid to admit problems and weaknesses. The critics and judges seem to come out of the walls when we do. However, it is unutterably sad to let your well-being and that of your family be controlled—not only by addiction but also by fear concerning the reaction of others. Courage is needed to face oneself, and then the world, with honesty.

Support is also crucial for those who live with a substance abuser. The families of substance abuse victims must also obtain help in breaking out of the destructive patterns that the user's addiction have created. If you are at a loss to find help, call the nationwide hotline run by the National Institute on Drug Abuse (1-800-662-HELP). A family doctor or pastor can also provide you with information.

Whether you recognize yourself as an abuser or live with one, ongoing support is important. Addiction is a prison for both the abuser and those with whom he or she lives. Do not allow yourself to be locked in such a prison. Professional help and loving support can free you.

THIRTY-TWO

What Is Codependency?

C ODEPENDENCY IS A TERM YOU HEAR OFTEN TODAY. Though many people talk about it, it sometimes seems unclear whether they are all discussing the same thing. The word codependency appeared on the treatment scene in the late seventies, when it was used to describe people who were involved with someone who was chemically dependent. It was observed that those involved with chemically dependent people tended to develop unhealthy ways of coping, to the point where their own lives became unmanageable.

Codependent literally means "a partner in dependency." Descriptions of codependents run like these: "She devoted her life to making them happy." "Other people's moods control her emotions." "She tries to control their feelings." "She feels responsible when he's upset."

Earnie Larsen, a codependent specialist, defines codependency as, "those self-defeating, learned behaviors or character defects that result in a diminished capacity to initiate or participate in a loving relationship." According to his definition, and the extensive lists of characteristics some authors give, all of us are codependent in some way. Certainly we all act in ways that inhibit our participation in loving relationships. There do, however, seem to be people for whom codependency is more of a problem.

Codependent relationships are characterized by unspoken

175

rules which restrict the handling of a problem with someone who is dependent and needy. Examples of these rules are: no discussion of the problem, no expression of feelings, no visible conflict, no straightforward communication. Obviously then, the relationship is ruled by the problem. One person has the problem, the other person is the caretaker, the fixer, the solution-finder.

The result is usually a vicious cycle. First of all, caretaking of an adult implies he is incompetent. The response of the caretaker is to rescue the troubled person. Having rescued him, the caretaker usually feels angry at the one they have rescued for being such a mess, for needing so much help, and for his lack of appreciation for all the rescuer has done. This is followed by strong feelings of victimization, and feeling sorry for oneself.

A typical example is a woman married to an alcoholic. He fails to come home from work on time. He shows up late and drunk, falls into bed, and does not get up in time for work. The boss calls, and his wife covers for him by saying he is sick (rescue). The man sleeps late and wakes up sick and in a foul mood. The wife is angry that she is stuck with this brute and begins to nag and criticize (persecutor). Eventually she becomes depressed and feels sorry for herself, because after all she does for this man she gets nothing in return. And so it goes for years and years.

One of the major difficulties for Christians in dealing with codependency lies in the fact that much of the caretaking behavior of the codependent seems to be in keeping with scriptural guidelines. God tells us to be kind, not to be selfish, not to go around hurting others' feelings, and to consider others as more important than ourselves. Codependent behavior is often justified as falling within these guidelines. Christianity is used to support caretaking behavior.

What is right? How are we to decide what should govern our response to others? Should *their* needs dictate our response? Should *our* needs dictate our response? Has God given us guidelines that will help us answer these questions?

We must first understand why the codependent engages in caretaking kinds of behavior. At first glance it may appear that the reason is simply unselfishness, or the desire to be truly helpful. However, usually underlying the caretaker's behavior is a driving personal need for self-esteem. At the bottom, then, codependent behavior fulfills one's own needs. What appears to be unselfish, is not. It is a misguided attempt to take care of oneself. The results are destructive to both the codependent and the troubled person. Each is kept from being personally responsible.

What is to govern the Christian's relationships? Should I constantly be looking out for your needs, running to your rescue no matter what? Or should I continually look out for my needs, regardless of how that affects you? Paul tells us in 2 Corinthians 5:9 what is to govern everything we do. He says, "Therefore also we have as our ambition, whether at home or absent, to be pleasing to Him." If Paul is right, then our relationships are to be governed by what pleases God, not by another's needs or our own. What does please God in our relationships?

In answering this we need to remember that human nature tends to go to extremes, to swing back and forth between two poles. All of history bears this out. Though God's His-Story—i.e., the Bible—is often radical, it is always balanced. His Word cuts through the divisions we make and seems always to offer a new way. What does this Word say to us about relationships?

First, in keeping with what Paul said, all our relationships are to be ruled by the ambition of pleasing God. Every word, thought, and action are to please him. They are not for the purpose of meeting the approval of others, for building our self-esteem or that of another. Nor are they for getting someone out of a mess, or for making others happy. A clear grasp of this will help us see that what comes naturally to us in relationships, or what we feel comfortable with, is not necessarily what will please God. Our responses to others need to be brought continually before God and held up to the light of his Word. Is this what you would have me to do, God? Is this what would glorify Christ?

Second, God never wants us to do anything contrary to his Word. My behavior in relationship to others needs to be unselfish and caring, yes, but it also needs to be governed by the fact that my body is the temple of the Holy Spirit. If I continue to involve myself with others in ways that fail to care for the body and life God has given me, then I am wrong. I am responsible before God for how I run my life. I will answer to him for how I have cared for my body. He will not excuse me from his standards because I was too busy running around picking up the pieces of someone else's life.

Third, Ephesians 4:15 gives us a good balance regarding our behavior in relationships. Paul says we are to "deal truly in love." Truth is often harsh and ugly. Truth exposes and confronts. Truth reveals consequences and does not hide. Our relationships are to be handled in truth. Love is patient, kind, and endures. Love extends grace. Love is not critical. Love is gentle. Jesus was the embodiment of these two things; he was "mercy and truth met together." He never compromised truth, yet he never ceased to be loving. Love that is exercised without truth is not loving. Truth exercised without love is not true.

How does this apply to codependency? Truth is hidden in rescuing. It is never loving to weaken others, which is exactly what we do when we continue to cover for their mistakes. A mother who lies for her son when he fails to do his homework has been neither truthful nor loving. She has crippled her son. All behavior has consequences, and to interfere in that cause and effect process is demeaning. Part of the dignity God has given to man is seen in the fact that what man does matters; it has effects. God did not prevent the consequences of Adam and Eve's choice, and we today continue to have to face the consequences of our choices. He does, however, deal with us lovingly while we face those consequences. We see him responding the same way to our individual sin. Whenever I sin, there is a consequence. Yet while I face the result of that choice, God meets me there in love. Obviously, God's response as seen in Christ's death is the ultimate expression of that.

We are called to be like Christ. Our responses to others need to be governed by the ambition of being pleasing to God. We please him when both truth and love are evident in our behavior toward others. That means we will not weaken others or demean them by covering for them, by rescuing them, by helping them escape the consequences of their behavior. We will then be walking in truth.

At the same time, we will not nag or criticize or wrongfully blame them for the condition of our lives. We will be patient with them as God works in their lives through the consequences of their choices. We will then be walking in love. We do not measure our obedience to God by another's approval or pleasure. Rather, we are to measure our obedience by the Word of God. As we change our sights from others and their problems, to God and his standards, the delicate balance we have discussed will become more and more clear to us. Our focus will not be on other people or our circumstances, no matter how difficult or painful they may be. Our goal will be to grow continually in our ability to find our self-esteem in Christ and his infinite love for us. It follows that we will then honor him by demonstrating both respect and compassion for others.

Part Five

A Woman and Her Emotions

THIRTY-THREE

Anger

EMOTIONAL REACTIONS ARE OFTEN SIGNALS that we need to listen carefully to what is going on inside us. Anger is one of these. When something happens and we feel anger rise within us, we need to stop and listen. Unfortunately, we are all too often unwilling to listen because anger frightens us. We know that if we express anger it could result in the disapproval of others. People often respond in ways that suggest our anger was not legitimate, so we end up feeling wrong or bad. Another reason that anger frightens us is because anger tells us things are not right. Something seems wrong or unjust. If we really listen to the anger, then change will be in order, and most of us fear change.

Kay frequently felt angry when her husband did not finish tasks around the house. Invariably, he would get started on something and stop before it was completed. She would get furious, and begin to nag and complain. Her husband would respond defensively and purposely refuse to finish the job. Kay spent most of the first six years of her marriage angry. By the time she came to see me, she had a string of unresolved issues and deep bitterness toward her husband.

Kay's anger clearly signaled to her that something was amiss. She relied on her husband to do the jobs he felt were his, to finish them, and do them well. Her husband failed to meet her expectations, which were not unrealistic or demanding. Her disappointment was justified and not surprising. The problem was not in Kay's feelings about the situation. It really arose out of how she chose to express those feelings. Her disappointment led her into criticism and judgment of her husband, and his anger led him into defensiveness and a refusal to change. The result was a vicious cycle which continued for many years. But what other options did Kay have?

Again, anger is a symptom, a signal that something is wrong. If we respond to a situation with anger it usually means that something did not happen the way we thought it should. That is not necessarily the same as saying that I am mad just because I did not get my own way. I may have wanted to see someone treated with justice, when instead he received injustice. This would cause me to be angry. Or I may have longed to see a reconciliation take place, or someone accorded respect, or a change take place that was clearly what God intended. Even Jesus responded with anger when God's house was used for greedy and selfish purposes. To say that we respond with anger when things do not go as we thought they should is to acknowledge that anger was the appropriate response.

On the other hand, sometimes we react in anger because our expectations or desires are unreasonable or even wrong. A woman who expects never to be criticized or hurt will often be angry because her expectations are unrealistic. A leader who demands that her followers always do what she wants will be sadly disappointed and become angry. A driver who expects traffic patterns to accommodate her need for speed will become angry very quickly. In these cases anger hits because we simply have been selfish and demanding. When our expectations are unreasonable, we set ourselves up to be continually frustrated and angry. Anger always indicates that things are other than we want them to be. Our first task, then, is to figure out whether or not what we expected was justified and within reason.

The man who batters his wife because she either burned

the dinner or expressed an opinion that differed from his is inappropriately angry. That is obvious. However, discerning the appropriateness of our own anger is not always so easy. Sometimes we are certain of our right to feel anger, as well as our expression of it. Then, as time elapses, we are able to see that our underlying motives were indeed wrong and perhaps selfish or self-justifying. What about our anger when friends are late for a dinner engagement, or when our child disobeys for the third time, or our husband fails to mention an appointment that affects our schedule? It is very easy to assume that we are justified in our response, and we are usually quite adept at finding reasons to support our conclusions.

Proverbs is full of admonitions to exercise caution when we are angry. The ability to restrain our tongues is praised over and over again. Proverbs 14:29 says, "He who is slow to anger has great understanding." The reason for the statement is obvious. As soon as anger takes over, our ability to think is clouded. We become ruled by emotion and cannot discern well. If we are slow to anger, then we have more time in which to gain an understanding about the situation we are facing. For example, if a husband walks in late for dinner and is immediately greeted with a tirade, his wife never has the opportunity to learn why he was late. Perhaps he stopped at the scene of an accident to help those who were injured or his boss had called him into his office for an unexpected meeting. There might have been any number of unforeseen circumstances. Had she been slow to anger, she would have had an understanding about the circumstances that she was unaware of. Instead, she allowed her anger to lead her.

If anger is a signal for something that is not readily apparent, then the ability to pause and read the signal becomes even more vital. It may be giving us a clue about something inside us, or it may be telling us something about the situation, or perhaps both. We need to ask ourselves some questions when anger threatens to overtake us. Exactly what am I angry about? What really is the problem? What options do I have regarding my response, and what do I hope to accomplish by it? How can I express myself so as not to put the other person on the defensive?

If after a careful look at ourselves we find that we are often inappropriately angry, then we need to recognize that our anger is probably indicative of a problem unrelated to the immediate circumstances. For example, a woman who found herself very angry with men in situations where it was clear to all that she was overreacting, realized that the real issue was a rape she experienced many years ago. The emotional turmoil it had caused had never been resolved. Her buried anger about the rape spilled over continually into her present relationships with men, causing her to react with rage to the slightest injustice. Buried anger of this sort often requires the help of a professional to understand and learn how to handle.

If, on the other hand, we are typically angry in appropriate ways, but the results of our expressions of anger tend to end in frustration, then we need to look at how we are choosing to show our anger. Anger that is expressed in statements beginning with "You always..." or "You never...," often generates defensive reactions from others and creates distance. Any time we express ourselves in ways that inherently carry judgment, we will elicit a response that is defensive.

Return to our original example of Kay who expressed her anger in words of complaint and dissatisfaction. The hidden message, which her husband heard quite clearly, was that he was inadequate. Such a message was heard as an attack against his person, rather than a clear statement of Kay's feelings and needs. It was important for Kay to understand that she was interpreting her husband's unfinished work as an expression of his lack of concern for her. If he loved her enough he would do what she wanted. She was very threatened by this seeming lack of love, and her fear pushed her into going after him in negative ways. Once Kay was able to see that her husband's unfinished work was his problem, a difficulty that he struggled with at the office as well, she was able to pull back from her attacks. She could see that he did not leave jobs uncompleted because he did not love her, but because he had a hard time finishing things. Understanding this helped free Kay to work *with* her husband on this problem, rather than *against* him. She found ways to encourage her husband, rather than criticizing him or stepping in to do the work for him, both of which made him feel inadequate.

To handle anger in this way requires insight and great honesty with ourselves, plus self-discipline, and a willingness to try to understand one another. All these things take time, which is exactly what anger does not allow. Anger pushes us to quick action and impulsive responses, making restraint difficult. Rather than learning to control our anger, most of us just do what comes naturally. Many of us, because of our fear of anger, and bolstered by a false understanding of what God's Word says about it, hide behind pretense. We say that we do not feel angry. We smile and pretend things are all right when they are not. Sometimes we respond by becoming silent, or acting tearful or hurt. These are often ways of cloaking anger. We are being dishonest in our relationships and when we do this we bury our anger until we have a veritable storehouse of it. Frequently this buried anger affects us physically, and becomes manifest in such genuine disorders as colitis, ulcers, depression, and sleep disorders.

Another common response, rather than burying our anger, is expressing it freely and without restraint. We are harsh in our relationships with others, often under the guise of just "telling it like it is." We are blunt and show insufficient care in the way we handle the feelings of others. We are proud of the fact that others never have to wonder what we are thinking. We say that if they cannot handle the truth, well then, that's their problem. This response is as inappropriate as the opposite. Neither will bring about the result we want, which is a harmonious solution to the problem, whatever it is.

When anger signals that something is wrong we need to heed it. We must first determine what is wrong and where. Having done so, we then need to see that we have choices about how we will respond. We can ignore it and hope it will go away. We can respond harshly by criticizing and attacking the other person. Or we can, based on a thoughtful understanding of the situation, look for an honest and responsible answer that shows care regarding the needs and feelings of the one we are angry with.

As we seek to find this balance in our relationships with others, then I think we will be fulfilling the command "be angry and yet do not sin." This command makes it clear that anger in itself is not necessarily wrong, and that there is a way for us to communicate our anger without sin. Being careful, having a listening ear, and expressing love for the one who has injured us will help guide us in finding that response.

THIRTY-FOUR

Should I Feel So Guilty?

P AUL TOURNIER, the Swiss psychiatrist, said, "There is no life without conflict; no conflict without guilt." This is true because everything we do involves making a choice and to choose one thing means we must let go of another. The result is often guilt. When we choose to stay home rather than attend a meeting, we feel guilty. When we choose to relax rather than work on a job, we feel guilty. When we choose to work on a book chapter rather than make muffins for our family, we feel guilty! The student who chooses to study hard and make A's often feels guilty around class-mates who have not done well. Add to this the conflicts beyond our control which produce guilt. For example, when a parent dies, a child responds with guilt. Or if a person loses his job, the person who fired him feels guilty. Often a parent whose child has made wrong choices experiences terrible guilt. Many people end up seeking counseling because of intolerable guilt.

People often have difficulty differentiating between true guilt and false guilt. What do these terms mean? Is it possible to feel guilty, without having committed any wrong? Throughout the eighteen years I have been a psychologist, I have seen many people who were crippled by false guilt. Women who were victims of incest as tiny girls often carry a deep sense of guilt, as if they were at fault. Mothers whose babies were born with a deformity often feel responsible, even though they were very careful of their health during pregnancy.

Patty was burdened down with false guilt when she consulted me. She had grown up with an alcoholic father, and what is often referred to as a "ghost mother." Her father was abusive, both physically and sexually. While he had committed incest with her and treated her cruelly since she was three, her mother had turned a blind eye to the situation, making no effort to intervene. Patty carried a great sense of guilt about what her father had done. She believed that if she had somehow behaved better, made better grades, or been more obedient, her father would not have "had" to punish her. There were, of course, real things she had done wrong as a child, as every child does, and she used these to bolster her case against herself. She had a twisted understanding of responsibility and the consequences of behavior and guilt. It took a long time for the two of us to unravel these things, so she could find freedom from a cruel and unnecessary burden of guilt. Though the guilt she carried was false, it was every bit as real and painful as true guilt.

Helping to unravel guilty feelings is a complex problem. Not only are there many people who carry great burdens unnecessarily, there are also those who have committed wrong, yet do not feel any guilt at all. Still others have transgressed, feel guilt, yet want to name the guilt something else, so as not to face responsibility for what they have done.

I remember a patient who was quite depressed and felt guilty all the time. She kept insisting that both her depression and guilt resulted from feelings of low self-esteem, not from an appropriate guilt over a wrong she had done. However, as she told her story, it became clear that this was not the case. Both her depression and guilt had begun due to her sexual involvement with a married man. She insisted that one thing had nothing to do with the other. She was correct in her diagnosis of low self-esteem, for that was indeed a problem area for her. But she was incorrect in say-ing that it was the reason she felt guilty. She felt guilty because she had done wrong.

To make the situation even more complex, there are also those who have done wrong, say they feel guilt, yet never seem to face their culpability. Instead, they continue to almost wallow in their guilt. It is far better to have a true sense of guilt, the kind which motivates us to examine our-selves, and to change.

What then are we to do with our guilt? It would seem that we cannot rely on the feeling itself to be accurate. Fear and self-deception often distort our view so we cannot think clearly about ourselves. Truly, "the heart is deceitful above all things…"

There are, I believe, at least three very unreliable ways we often use to determine whether or not we are guilty. This is not to say that these things should not be considered, or even used as guides; but they must not be our final authority. The first is to decide that we are guilty because we feel guilty. I have already shown how easily we can arrive at false conclu-sions by following this line of thought. Feelings are variable, and often not responsive to rational thought. They are not a reliable way of making a final judgment about anything. The child whose mother dies feels very guilty. Maybe if he had not disobeyed, or been a better boy, then she would still be alive. His feelings of guilt are powerful and may last well into adult life. To say that, because he has those feelings therefore he must in some way be responsible for his mother's death, is both cruel and illogical. Obviously, feel-ings alone cannot be the determinant.

The second way many of us decide whether or not we are guilty is through the judgment of others. All of us fear human judgment, and with good reason. We ourselves often judge each other with harshness and unfairness. We deal with this fear of judgment in one of two ways. Some of us automatically assume that if others judge us to be wrong, then it must be so, and we do not examine ourselves to see if they are correct. If others say I am inadequate or wrong, then I accept the decision. A second response that can arise out of our fear, is to assume that others do not know very much, their intelligence is inferior to mine and that therefore, I do not have to consider or evaluate their judgments or criticisms. In both instances, it is the judgment of others that determines our response, not whether or not we are actually guilty of something. We seem to have a "knee-jerk" reaction to the opinions of others. Their judgment, and our fear of that judgment, inhibit us from examining ourselves, and trying to assess whether or not we are truly guilty.

A third way is to work backwards from the circumstances. If something traumatic happens, we assume the blame. Loss of a job, death of a spouse, or a car accident, any of these can make us feel we did something wrong. We see circumstances as punishment, and life simply as a cause-effect struggle. Certainly behavior has consequences, but at the same time we live in a twisted, irrational world due to sin. If I smoke excessively and get lung cancer, then yes, I am culpable. But if I lose my temper with my husband before he leaves for work, and then he is injured by a drunk driver on his way to work, then no, it is not my fault. However, if I were to reason backwards from the circumstances, I would feel like assuming the guilt in both cases.

If I am not to rely on feelings, the judgments of others, or my circumstances to decide whether or not I am guilty, then how am I to make the determination? True guilt is, of course, that which results from God's judgment, not man's. It is not myself or another who can rightly determine my guilt, but God himself. However, we have seen how hopelessly entangled our minds can become, so our task of determining true guilt is not easy. If the only just judge is God, then I must go to him to decide whether or not I am guilty.

My life must continually be lived and examined in the light of God's word. That will be easier to do at some times than at others. I don't always want to hear that word, and sometimes I will misunderstand it and excuse or blame myself wrongly. At other times it will just be unclear for awhile. It is important to remember that this is a growth process in the life of the Christian. There is no simple formula for living a guilt-free life. Nor is there an easy answer for how to determine the validity of the guilt we feel. It involves constantly going back to God and looking at our lives, asking him to sharpen our insights so that we see ourselves more and more clearly.

If we are carrying a heavy burden of guilt, we need to assume that something is awry and needs our attention. The feelings may indicate that we are wrong about something, or they may not. But they certainly indicate a problem exists. Sometimes guilt is a symptom of a severe depression or another psychological problem which will require the help of a professional. If it is the result of another's judgment, we need to consider and evaluate the criticism. Often others are able to see us more clearly than we see ourselves. I have frequently found that even when others have misunderstood and judged wrongly, a close look at myself has resulted in growth. When trauma occurs, we cannot automatically assume guilt, but we do need to consider whether or not our actions have brought a problem about. Human beings are complex, and we are not as wise as we would like to think. We see something, and make a judgment of ourselves or another, and guilt is determined. How often we are wrong!

If we are truly so complex, and if discerning between false guilt and true is not easy, then it follows that we should be very careful in our judgments and criticisms of others. This restraint is something we all find very difficult. We are so conscious of the wrongs of others. Even the disciples fell into the trap of judging others, and Jesus responded similarly to both. In Luke 13, Jesus asked the disciples whether they thought that certain Galileans had been killed because they were greater sinners than other Galileans. Or, on the second occasion, whether those on whom a tower fell were worse than others in the city. In both cases Jesus said no, "But unless *you* repent, you will all likewise perish." Rather than focusing on the problems of others, and hypothesizing about their culpability, Jesus turned the focus on the disciples.

God always says that the important thing is the state of our relationship with him. Whether we feel intensely guilty, whether others have judged us, or whether we are keenly aware of wrong done by others—our concern should be the same: What is the state of *my* relationship with God? It is there that I can determine whether or not my feelings have led me rightly. It is there that I can decide whether or not the judgments of others are correct. And it is there that I can learn how to respond to wrong done by others.

Certainly, whenever we find ourselves guilty before God, confession and acceptance of God's forgiveness must follow. Confession is the door to freedom from our guilt. This is true both before God and before others. We have all experienced as children the awareness of our wrongdoing and how, when it went unconfessed, it controlled our relationship to our parents. We felt anxious and fearful, and wanted to hide from them. Confession brought freedom.

In the case of human parents, forgiveness sadly does not always follow. However, with God we are assured of forgiveness and freedom from guilt. When we have wronged another we risk a rejection of our confession. With God there is no condemnation. Our thinking often requires some hard work in this area. We think pretense is better than confession, we think God will never forgive, and we think forgiveness is somehow purchased by good behavior.

Finally, we do not need to be afraid of guilt. It can serve the same purpose that pain does in the physical realm. Pain in my hand indicates that the fire is hot, so that I know to remove my hand and not burn it. Guilt, and its accompanying pain, can be a similar indicator. At times it can even be considered a gift. Without the push that guilt gives us, how often would we seek God and submit ourselves to the light of his Word?

All of us are guilty before God. All of us are guilty of specific wrongs throughout our lives. The grace of God is available for just that reason. Let us make use of it again and again, knowing his grace is infinite. Not only is that grace available when we have been wrong, it continues to be available when we avoid facing the truth about ourselves. And it is also there to free us from the unnecessary guilt we often carry.

Whether you are struggling with false or true guilt (and we all must deal with both), keep in mind that in either case, guilt is the one thing that brings you face to face with the grace of God. And what a marvelous gift that is!

THIRTY-FIVE

I'm Filled with Bitterness

M ANY THINGS IN LIFE seem almost calculated to cause bitterness. We live in a world that is often grossly unfair and full of pain. Many people face terrible tragedies such as the death of a child, a wrenching divorce, the unwarranted loss of a job, or vicious slander—to name just a few of what Hamlet calls "the thousand natural shocks that flesh is heir to." The list is as varied as anyone's circumstances. Most of us have encountered situations which have made us bitter, and we know that ridding ourselves of this insidious emotion is extremely difficult.

Jane was bitter toward a woman in her church, who had been a close friend for six years. This woman had betrayed her by talking against her and distorting some things Jane had said. They had always shared many things, and Jane was afraid she would be betrayed by her again. The woman had refused to talk with her about what she had said or why, and Jane was bitter. Angry thoughts about the situation occupied her mind most of the time.

But what exactly is bitterness and how can we deal with it? The word bitter literally means "to bite," and indeed, a bitter experience is one that bites into our very being. It is painful to the mind, and has a sharpness, a sting, to it. If you have ever been around people who are bitter you can hear that sharpness in their words and tone of voice. Anger is certainly a part of bitterness, as are grief and feelings of spite. Bitterness that is allowed to continue becomes rancor, which occurs when we feel malice or ill will toward another person.

How does being bitter affect us? I think it causes a twisting and distorting of the personality of anyone who allows the bitterness to fester inside. First of all, bitterness begins to take center stage in a person's life. Jane was dwelling on the betrayal by her friend, and, by her own admission, she thought about it most of the time. She was consumed by her anger at the injustice, by her grief over the loss of their friendship, and ultimately, she found herself wishing ill for her former friend.

A second result is that as bitterness assumes control, our perspective becomes skewed. Not only does our perspective about the circumstances become altered, but eventually our outlook on others as well. In the beginning it will just affect our view of the one who has wronged us. But then we tend to forget the good in the relationship, and, because of this, it ends up being reduced to the betrayal alone. When we let this happen we have added to our own loss by denying ourselves the memory of what was good. From there the bitterness begins to infect our perspective of others as our trust level decreases, and we begin to define them as "enemy." The bitterness becomes a pre-existing condition to any new relationship we form. It causes us to start out new relationships in a twisted way. Bitter people often begin by telling about their painful experience, looking for their new friend to justify their bitterness. The retelling of the story is a test to see if the new person is "on our side," if she is really a friend, or an enemy.

Third, bitterness affects all of our reactions and emotions. We may find ourselves reacting with anger more frequently, and criticism and judgment of others will come more easily. Our heightened sensitivity to the wrong done to us and the fact that we cannot let go of it, will make us more quick to see wrong in how others behave in all situations. We may find our reactions becoming more negative, and we may begin to feel anger toward more people for wrongs we perceive, whether our perception is true or not. This results in our speaking maliciously about others. The results are ironic because we become the kind of person against whom we harbor such bitterness in the first place! We carry this acrimony for things spoken against us, and that malice, if held onto, leads us to speak harshly and critically of others. Thus we are made over into the image of that which controls us.

One of the most striking examples of this is Miss Havisham in Charles Dickens' *Great Expectations.* In her bitterness over a wedding that never happened, her life essentially stopped. She spent her days closeted in the house filled with things left as they were the day of the wedding. Dust, cobwebs, and old age ensued, but Miss Havisham remained as she was. Her house became a house of death, controlled by her grief and bitterness. That is what bitterness can do to us, if we get mired in it and cease to grow. We produce death, rather than life, and we are controlled by the sadness and injustice of the past. We become unable to experience the joy of the present and are denied the hope we might have of the future.

A final result of bitterness is the effect that it has on those around us. This is graphically illustrated for us in Hebrews 12:15: "See to it that no one comes short of the grace of God; that no root of bitterness springing up causes trouble, and by it many be defiled." The picture is that of a root, the tentacles of which reach up and entwine many. So bitterness not only consumes our whole being, it reaches further, and infects the lives of others.

I am sure you have been around someone whose life was controlled by bitterness. Her conversation is harsh, angry, and critical, and she is totally self-centered. It is very hard to maintain a forgiving and gentle spirit when we are involved with such a person. One of the reasons is that life too often seems unfair. And since we are all surrounded by sinners, we have many reminders of hurtful situations. When we are around a bitter person we are more aware of these negative realities, making it easier for us to become critical and judgmental also. We, too, begin to feel justified in our anger toward those who have hurt us. The tentacles of bitterness have reached out and touched us as well. You can easily see how this scenario could multiply!

So what are we to do? If indeed life comes off looking unfair and we all meet with bitter experiences, how are we to keep from becoming bitter people? Jane's friend truly did betray her. What she did was wrong and hurtful. She attacked and twisted Jane's confidences with devastating results. To be betrayed by one to whom we have made ourselves vulnerable is deeply painful. And to lose a friend we have loved and felt loved by is a very great loss.

How could Jane—or how can you—keep from becoming bitter in the midst of pain and loss? It is important to see that the choice is not between simply hanging onto the pain with bitterness, or pretending that everything is all right. Certainly we do not want to be bitter, but neither do we want to pretend that something does not hurt when it does. It is striking that the writer of both Ephesians and Hebrews, begins his statements about bitterness with "See to it that..." and "Let all... be put away..." This is similar to the admonition in Proverbs 4:23, 25: "Watch over your heart with all diligence, for from it *flow* the springs of life. Let your eyes look directly ahead, and let your gaze be fixed straight in front of you."

All of these imply choice and suggest that diligence is necessary in the tending of our hearts and spirits. We are told: do not allow, do not watch, or you will let. But if diligence is needed, then activity is also required. We are not to be passive regarding what we allow to reside in our hearts and minds. Diligence, watching out, or guarding against are all soldier-like qualities. We are to have a soldier-like attitude about our hearts and minds. We are to monitor what we allow to reside there, and we are not passively to allow harmful thoughts to come in and take up residence.

Suppose you have been terribly hurt by a friend and the pain you are experiencing runs very deep. What are you allowing to occupy your mind as a result of that pain? The pain does not have to determine what you think. Pain does not have to lead inevitably to bitterness, nor do you have to deny the pain in order to avoid the bitterness. Christ encountered great pain during his time on earth, yet we see no bitterness in him toward those who inflicted that pain.

How do you guard your heart and mind? You must not welcome thoughts of anger, malice, and revenge or those of judgment and criticism. Actively guard against those. Be vigilant, and as they enter, get rid of them. Do not dwell on them, do not nurture them, do not excuse them. That may require battling them every five minutes at first, and that will be particularly hard if bitterness already has a foothold. Your bitterness will be fed if you fix your mind on the circumstances that gave it birth. But you are not to feed it, nor are you to let it take up residence in your mind.

What *is* to fill our minds? We cannot effectively remove something from our minds unless we put something else in its place, because it will simply return to fill the empty space, leaving us defeated. Paul, the writer to the Hebrews, says, "See to it that no one falls short of the grace of God..." He adds, "And be kind to one another, tender-hearted, forgiving each other, just as God in Christ also has forgiven you" (Ephesians 4:32).

The alternative we are given, instead of bitterness, is the grace of God as evidenced in the cross of Christ. The point is, I believe, that worldly trials can darken our minds and eclipse the one thing that is to be central, the atoning work of Jesus Christ. The busyness of life, the suffering of life, and the questions of life all pull us away from him who is to rule our hearts and minds. A friend's betrayal can be just such a magnet, absorbing and controlling our thoughts, until we think, act, and relate with bitterness. However, we can instead think, act, and relate out of the work of Christ. How else can we possibly be kind, tender-hearted, and forgiving in a world that is so often unfair and full of pain? We cannot.

We are instructed to watch over our hearts and not allow bitterness to live there. At the same time, we must "Let your eyes look directly ahead, and let your gaze be fixed straight in front of you" (Proverbs 4:25). Our focus invariably will direct us. If the focus is a friend's betrayal, then our reaction to that betrayal will run our life. If it is an unfair boss, or a grievous loss, then our reaction to that will also control our life. If, however, it is the cross of Christ, then our response to his great love will control our life.

Once my patient, Jane, was able to find freedom from her bitterness, she tried again to talk with her friend about the hurt she felt. This proved to be wise and helpful, and it was good that her initial reaction was under control before she did it. There are many bitter experiences in life where that kind of conciliatory meeting is not feasible, but Jane was fortunate to have the opportunity for greater resolution.

One of the reasons it is good to talk to the people whom we have been bitter against is because it affords them the opportunity to ask for forgiveness, to learn from their mistake, and to some degree, to right the wrong they have done. To refuse to talk with them is to deprive that person of this chance. Sometimes they may refuse, or sometimes they may respond with great defensiveness. If we have truly gone into the encounter without bitterness, we will not try to force an agreement or apology. Our purpose in talking is to afford them the opportunity for growth through an understanding of the effect of their actions. Regardless of the outcome, we need not only to forgive them for the original offense, but for any defensiveness our attempt at resolution brings.

Is any of this easy? Of course not. Accepting responsibility for our attitudes and actions is always difficult. We want to justify what we do and how we feel, and we are experts at deluding ourselves. Having faced ourselves, and having faced where we are wrong in our response to injustice, it is equally difficult to bring about lasting change. Fighting against bitterness is not a one-time battle. The odds are we will not get down on our knees, pray about it, and then get up and find it gone. Not that God isn't capable of such a miracle, but he usually works only in due time, and he requires us to persevere with difficult things.

Bitterness is an enemy that will try to deflect us from our goal to be conformed to the image of Christ, and thereby mold us into its own image. We must fight bitterness as a soldier fights an enemy. Winning that fight will reward us with the freedom to act out of love, regardless of circumstances.

THIRTY-SIX

I'm So Lonely

S EVERAL YEARS AGO JEAN CAME TO SEE ME, overwhelmed by loneliness, especially in her marriage. She had children, but did not feel close to them. Though she had been involved in a church for many years, her friendships there seemed superficial, even though her help had always seemed welcomed and she had often assisted people in need. Yet relationships had never been long-lasting and she wondered why others, including her husband, seemed to avoid closeness with her.

Loneliness can be a terrible thing because human beings need and desire companionship. God himself says it is not good for us to be alone. Proverbs tells us that "two are better than one; for when the one shall fall, the other shall pick him up." Children who grow up neglected and without companionship in their homes develop severe problems. People do indeed need people all their lives. Most of us recognize this and are continually seeking ways to develop relationships. When our efforts fail, we feel lonely, and if our loneliness continues, we can become despairing.

There are two types of loneliness I would like to consider. The first is the loneliness that is the direct result of circumstances. A single missionary at a remote station will be very lonely, or a child who is transplanted midyear into a new school setting will be lonely. A man or woman in a top leadership position might also experience a kind of loneliness. These instances illustrate the loneliness that arises out of circumstances. It "goes with the territory," so to speak. It does not necessarily reflect the relationship style or personality of the one experiencing it. Even a woman who may be expertly skilled in relating to others, and has had great success knowing others in a deep way, may encounter loneliness because of the nature of her life or position. Knowing her loneliness is circumstantial will not necessarily lessen its impact, nor will it make the problem easier to handle. Though we may be able to think about this kind of loneliness differently and not blame ourselves for its presence in our lives, loneliness feels the same, whatever the reason for it.

The second kind of loneliness is self-induced. It results from the way an individual responds (or fails to respond) to others. Something in the personality of the individual or in his style of relating, keeps others at a distance.

Jean was struggling with that kind of loneliness. As we talked about her life and relationships, she discovered that she had gotten into the habit of gossiping and was constantly speaking against others. She often spoke against her own husband in conversations with other women and frequently criticized others in the church for how they handled their lives. As a result, no one felt safe with her. The fact that she spoke so freely against her husband, as well as others, caused people to keep their distance. They made the assumption, correct I am sure, that she would at some later date, talk about them as well.

Jean's constant criticism of others also communicated that she thought of herself as superior. This was not really the case; in fact, she felt very inferior to those around her. Negative criticism implies judgment and can be destructive. Feeling judged makes most people immediately defensive— and they feared Jean would judge them—so they kept their distance. Being distant from others was exactly what Jean did not want, yet she was, by her very actions, causing it.

We also learned, as we explored further, that Jean behaved that way with others because she in fact feared *their* judgment, and the rejection that could follow. Jean had grown up under a very severe father, who had criticized everything about her. He always found her inadequate, and because of this, she was afraid of relationships. She very much wanted closeness with others, and at the same time, she was afraid of it. Relationships would, on the one hand, fulfill her need for closeness. But on the other hand, they frightened her because she assumed they would lead to criticism and rejection. The posture Jean had taken toward others enabled her to meet both her need for distance and relationship simultaneously. Once she began to understand what she was doing, she was able to relate in a more successful way. She knew that she desired closeness, and though she also feared rejection, knew she had to learn to face others with the courage needed to risk the rejection that is always possible when we reach out to others.

Courage is required by all of us in order to truly maintain honest and lasting relationships with others. It demands courage to be faithful to another, to face our faults, to forgive others, and to choose not to run or hide in some way. It is human nature to hide. This has been evident since Adam and Eve's initial response to God after the Fall, and we continue to fight against this tendency in our relationships.

We all have different ways of hiding. Some of us hide behind silence, others behind gossip, and some behind anger. Some of us hide behind boredom or busyness; others of us use reading or some hobby to maintain distance. Some use humor, others knowledge, and still others, arrogance. We engage in these behaviors because we are afraid and they seem to protect us from rejection. However, they also distance us from others, and so we are lonely.

As Jean came to understand what she was doing and why, she realized that her loneliness was not the fault of others as she had thought. She realized that she herself had caused it by the way she related to others. That was a freeing thought, because then she knew that she could choose not to be lonely anymore. As she chose to reach out to others without criticism and judgment, they in turn began to respond to her and wanted to know her better.

When any of us experience loneliness, we must first give ourselves and our circumstances a good, hard look. It might be helpful to talk with one or two others about how they perceive us. "Do you see me acting in ways that push others away?" Many times we will see that we have inadvertently brought the experience on ourselves. There are behaviors and attitudes that we need to change if we want to clear the way for the development of healthy, productive relationships. As much as we desire closeness, we are also afraid of it and our behavior usually accommodates both our fear and our desire. The result is that we give others a double message. They too are afraid, and so they keep their distance.

As we come to see how we push others away or, at least, give them a double message, then we can take steps to act differently. Most people find this process somewhat frightening because it is usually fear of some kind which causes us to keep our distance in the first place. It means reaching out to others, showing an interest in their lives, and learning to listen actively. It is hard to do this when we fear rejection or feel inferior.

What about those times when our loneliness is a direct result of our circumstances? It does not usually lessen the pain just to realize that it is "not our fault." The longing for companionship is just as great. In that situation we need to handle the loneliness the way we would any kind of suffering. This is not to say that those who have perhaps caused their own loneliness are not suffering. They certainly are! However, there are tangible things they can probably do to alter their situation. When the loneliness is due to circumstances which cannot be changed, then all we can work with is our own response to the environment.

What should our response be in the face of suffering? Volumes have been written on this subject, and I obviously cannot begin to even scratch the surface in a chapter. Let me just offer a few thoughts for those who are overwhelmed with the loneliness of their situations, with no relief in sight. An important thing to remember is that no matter how hemmed in we feel by circumstance, there are always options regarding our response. We cannot always choose our circumstances, for often they are beyond our control. We can, however, choose what our response to those circumstances will be. Loneliness can be met with bitterness, self-pity, anger, and resistance. It can also be met with understanding, resilience, acceptance, and concentration on the task at hand. To respond to difficulty in this way requires just as much courage as does facing ourselves and learning new ways of relating. Courage is always necessary for facing hard things in appropriate ways, whatever the reason for their existence.

Peter talks about facing suffering in a courageous way when he says, "Therefore, let those also who suffer according to the will of God entrust their souls to a faithful Creator in doing what is right" (1 Peter 4:19). He is clearly talking about a suffering that God has ordained, rather than one that is self-imposed. He says we are to trust ourselves to God and get on with the task at hand.

This is hard to do, particularly when our emotions are in turmoil. Often we allow whatever is causing our suffering to consume us and to control our lives. We get so swallowed up by our difficulty, that we fail to focus on the task. It is very difficult when something hurts, not to let that become who we are. We experience this even with something so tiny as a paper cut. How aware we are of that little cut! How we fill our thoughts with it! We let it steal our minds away from where they ought to be. Clearly, it is even easier to fall prey to this when the pain is deep and no end is in sight. It takes tremendous mental discipline to focus on what we are called to do in spite of the pain that is tugging on our sleeve for attention.

Loneliness can cause deep suffering. It is a hard place to be. However, we do have the ability to determine our response to it. Have we caused it by the way we relate to others? Then courage is needed to face ourselves and learn new ways. Is it brought on by circumstances over which we have no control? Then courage is needed to enable us to trust ourselves to a faithful Creator and continue with the job at hand. Both of these responses will help us to handle the circumstances of our lives in a productive way.

THIRTY-SEVEN

I'm Overwhelmed with Grief

M ARY HAD NO SOONER SAT DOWN in my office than she started crying. "I promised myself I wouldn't do this, but I can't seem to stop. My friends are sick of me, and think I've shed enough tears. I guess I'm just weak or something."

As she told her story, Mary related the pain of the past six months with great emotion. Her daughter, Melanie, had left home the night of her high school graduation to celebrate with friends. There was a terrible car accident, and Melanie was instantly killed. Mary was consumed by grief. She and her daughter had had a good relationship and had enjoyed each other. Everywhere Mary turned she was reminded of her loss. Her friends talked about their kids' summer jobs in preparation for college and it tore her apart. Every time Mary saw a car like the one her daughter was in, she felt overwhelmed. Church was impossible because it was full of Melanie's friends. Mary felt confused about God and why he had let this happen. Her husband was handling Melanie's death in silence, and did not want to hear anything his wife had to say. Brad, their son, was dealing with it by keeping himself busy and absent from the house as much as possible. Mary's friends, she thought, were tired of listening to her talk about it. She felt that something must be wrong with her that she wasn't feeling better by now.

211

The death of a loved one is devastating. Everything seems wrong and out of control. Nothing is the way we thought. Safety and security are smashed. We become disoriented. We feel lost because what was known is gone, and we could not prevent its going. We feel confused, preoccupied, and unable to make decisions. We forget to take care of ourselves. We question whether or not God is trustworthy. We feel depressed and have no energy for life. It is both a frightening and a frustrating time.

The trauma may be compounded by the reactions of others. People become impatient with how long we are taking to "get over it." They seem to respond as if life should have righted itself after a few weeks, or certainly after several months. We tend to respond by isolating ourselves, for fear others will think we are crazy or weak. Many people are uncomfortable around grief, which is a further encouragement toward isolation. We keep our mourning private, so as to avoid criticism and alienation by others. People are often complimentary of those who seem to bounce right back and say things to suggest that those who quit crying soon and return to life as if nothing had happened, are the strong ones. Others often say that the best way to deal with grief is to get busy and ignore it. Unfortunately, this often leads to making big decisions at a time when we are not thinking clearly. Many people have remarried quickly, gotten pregnant again as soon as possible, changed jobs or moved, just to avoid facing their loss. This simply adds to the stress. To avoid the pain of grieving is unhealthy.

Mourning is painful, and unless there is something wrong with us, most of us do not desire pain. However, to persist in ignoring pain is equally unhealthy. Our first response to loss is usually denial, so the urge to run or pretend is great. We cannot believe this is happening to us; it cannot be true. The first task for the mourner is to face the reality of the death. This is not an instantaneous acceptance, but one which occurs over time. For Mary, that process began at the hospital when she was required to identify her daughter. It continued as she had to face days that did not include the presence of her daughter, with the growing awareness that she was not just away somewhere.

As the reality of the loss sets in, anger begins to surface. Sometimes we are angry with ourselves—"If only I had not let her go." Sometimes we are angry with another, such as the driver of the other car. Often we are angry with God. For some of us this is very frightening, because we are expressing anger at a God we feel we cannot trust anymore. He seems untrustworthy because he has allowed such tragedy to enter our lives. So we become angry and afraid at the same time. It is often at this time that Christians feel like they have to isolate themselves, for they fear criticism from other Christians for being honest about their thoughts.

As time passes, we find we need to adjust to a radically different environment. We often do not realize how important someone was to us, until their absence makes it apparent. There are big gaps in our life emotionally, socially, and physically. We have lived with this person, and suddenly we have to learn to live without them. We do not know how to do this, and it takes time to learn.

Guilt is often prevalent as we remember all the things we did not do for or with the lost one. The thought of learning, at the age of sixty-five, how to live life without the person you have slept next to for forty years, is staggering. The thought of learning to live life without a child you have borne and raised, and whose future you looked forward to with hope and joy, is absolutely overwhelming. Certainly this is nothing any of us are capable of doing in a few months' time.

In spite of tremendous pain that feels it has no end, we can do two things that will help us heal. The first is to have supportive, nurturing people in our lives. Those who mourn need to be comforted. They need listening ears, shared tears, and the touch of another. One of the ways we progress through our mourning is by telling the story of the lost loved one and their death over and over. This helps us understand what has happened. It helps us to think clearly and to find ways to put our lives back together. If, for some reason, we cannot find this support from friends and family, then we need to consider participating in a grief support group. These can usually be found through a church or local hospital. Oftentimes, the groups are specialized. For example, there may be one especially for parents who have lost children to cancer, or for parents whose children were killed by drunk drivers.

The second way we can contribute to our own healing is by taking care of ourselves physically. When we experience great grief we tend to isolate ourselves from others. Those who are socially isolated are more likely to eat improperly, to not get exercise, and to keep odd hours. When we fail to care for ourselves, we add to our depression. A healthy routine is important to maintain. Sometimes that even means continuing to prepare for bed at the regular time, though we are unable to sleep. It is very easy to get into the habit of avoiding bedtime because we fear we cannot sleep. The result is that our days and nights get turned around, which feeds into our depression and confusion.

There are several warning signs to watch for; if these occur professional help is needed. It is not so much instances of these that indicate a problem, rather it is when they persist and cannot be shaken, that help should be sought. The first is recurrent thoughts of self-destruction. Most people experiencing grief will have feelings about life not being worth living, or that they would like to join the loved one. These are understandable thoughts. If however, we are consistently focusing on suicidal thoughts or making plans for how to kill ourselves, it is time to seek help.

A second warning sign is if you find yourself unable to care for your physical needs. Again, this is not uncommon for those who are grieving, particularly if they become some-what isolated. However, when you are consistently unable to care for yourself physically, help and support from others is necessary. This involves the willingness to share with others your struggles and needs, something many of us are afraid to do.

A third indicator of difficulty is long-term depression. Keep in mind that the mourning process takes a year or more, so we are not saying that we should assume that something is abnormal because we are sad for a long time. Anniversaries, such as birthdays, will continue to be difficult even after the mourning process is basically over. However, over time we can generally see changes that indicate healing is taking place. When a phase persists, and no relief comes, and there is no sign of moving on to the next stage, then out-side help should be sought. For example, numbness is an initial reaction to a death, but when we avoid grieving alto-gether, it is abnormal. Progressive social isolation, with no response to the interventions of friends is also indicative of the need for professional help. Severe depression into the second year or later requires professional intervention.

Mourning is an adaptive process. If we look carefully at individuals who mourn, we see that grief work serves a function. Its function is to free the individual from some of the ties to the lost person. Anyone we lose who is significant to our lives leaves a void which hurts. They are missed for a long time. To deny our feelings and to prevent the normal process of grieving to occur is to keep ourselves from healing and learning how to reorganize our life so that it can go on. Sometimes people will invest a great deal of energy into not reorganizing their lives, as if to do so were somehow an insult to the lost loved one. The emotional and physical energy required to maintain life as if the loved one is not gone, is tremendous. The result is unhealthy, frustrating, and depressing. You will certainly never forget the one who is lost. However, as healing occurs your thoughts will cease to revolve around them. Your thinking will instead become more and more focused on the present and future.

For the Christian there is an added dimension, to both the struggle and healing. There may be more questions for us as Christians, because our ideas of God are often shaken by trauma. It is important to remember this as we listen to those who mourn. Their need to wrestle with their questions out loud is just as crucial as their need to express other feelings. We must not be quick to judge others' questions and doubts in time of trouble.

We need to remember we are creatures of time. We live in time; things happen to us in the context of time. Many scripture verses are concerned with comfort in the face of grief. We need to hear these with our hearts and minds. However, their application in our lives will take time, and as God is patient with us in our struggles, so we need to be patient with ourselves and others who are wrestling with their grief.

Christ was sent into this world to comfort those who mourn. Many scriptural passages indicate that God expects us to mourn in the face of death, and that he understands our grief. He has promised not only to comfort us, he has given us hope because of his victory over death. For the believer, there is knowledge that this life is not all there is. Death is the passageway to a more glorious life with God himself. It is Christ who continues to bring life out of death. He enables us, after our grieving is done, to touch other lives with the same comfort he gave to us: "Blessed be the God and Father of our Lord Jesus Christ, the Father of mercies and God of all comfort; who comforts us in our affliction so that we may be able to comfort those who are in any affliction with the comfort with which we ourselves are comforted by God" (2 Corinthians 1:3-4).

Though we both fight against and fear the pain of grief, it is both necessary and healing. We must allow it to happen if we are to go on, not permanently fixed in our grief. Those of us who are given the privilege of sharing another's pain, need to handle it with respect and love, and without judgment. We will not comfort with quick words and snap solutions. Comfort comes from the steady presence of one who loves and listens.

Other Books of Interest
from Servant Publications

How to Pray for Your Family and Friends
Quin Sherrer with Ruthanne Garlock

Quin Sherrer and Ruthanne Garlock have taught thousands
the keys to releasing God's power in their world through inter-
cession. Now they've combined their wisdom and experience to
help Christians make prayer a first rather than a last resort.

How to Pray for Your Family and Friends is full of practical
wisdom to help readers learn how to pray persistently and specif-
ically, how to base their prayers on scriptural promises, and how
to overcome barriers to effective prayer. *$8.95*

How to Stop Living for the Applause
Help for Women Who Need to Be Perfect
Holly G. Miller and Dennis E. Hensley

Some women live with hidden anxiety about failure. They set
incredibly high standards for themselves and believe that more is
always better.

But now there's help for over-achievers and perfectionists
whose patterns of thought and behavior cheat them out of the
peace and happiness they long for. Holly Miller and Dennis
Hensley explain how a woman can break out of self-destructive
tendencies and achieve balance without giving up the challenges
she enjoys. *$7.95*

Available at your Christian bookstore or from:
**Servant Publications • Dept. 209 • P.O. Box 7455
Ann Arbor, Michigan 48107**
Please include payment plus $1.25 per book
for postage and handling.
*Send for our FREE catalog of Christian
books, music, and cassettes.*